TRAVELLING HOPEFULLY

Pat Laing

Published under licence by Brown Dog Books, 7 Green Park Station, Bath BA1 1JB

ISBN 978-190305-635-7

Cover design by Kevin Rylands

Printed and bound by CPI Group (UK) Ltd, Croydon CR0 4YY

To my husband and family, without whom none of this would have happened.

Contents

Foreword

It should be remembered that in the 1960s, 1970s and 1980s there were no credit or debit cards, mobile phones, internet or even pre-packed sandwiches and bottled water. We survived.

Chapter 1

1964 – To Palma by plane

'Getting there is half the fun' was the much advertised slogan used by the Cunard Line in the 1950s. This book, if it does nothing else, emphatically disproves that statement – at least as far as my family and I are concerned.

For the first twenty-nine years of my life, travel was nothing but a great joy. I travelled quite extensively throughout the UK and to Spain, Italy, the Netherlands and the USA, mainly by train or boat, and then by air which, by the late 1950s, was becoming an economic alternative. My husband Wally, whom I married in 1959, was an equally enthusiastic traveller and we took full advantage of the various travel offers available. The arrival of our daughters, Jane in 1960 and Sarah in 1961, did nothing to lessen our desire to travel and we merely exchanged city-based holidays for those offering sun, sea and sand. In 1962 we booked a two-week stay in a hotel in Majorca. It was ideal, being situated a hundred yards from a five-mile stretch of sandy beach, with adults' and children's swimming pools and a play area with swings and slides set under the shade of trees. It also offered a standard of luxury in which, if it had existed in the UK at the time, we would have been hard-pressed to afford two glasses of lemonade, let alone a fortnight's full board for four. Spain in the early 1960s offered exceptionally good value for money. We travelled by air from our local airport and within a twenty-minute taxi ride were at our hotel. The ease of travel and facilities at the hotel persuaded us to book again for late spring in 1963, arriving home in time for the arrival of our third daughter, Katie.

Still full of enthusiasm for Majorca and this hotel, we booked it again for the following year, 1964. This was the holiday that was to change the pattern of our travel forever.

It all began smoothly enough. My parents dropped us off at our local airport and after a short wait we boarded our plane. It was a DC-4 – very popular in the early 1960s – and had four propeller engines. We were seated at the very front of the (one-class) accommodation. Wally sat in the front aisle seat with eleven-month-old Katie on his lap and two young girls, making their first flight, sitting in the middle and window seats. I was in the row immediately behind with Jane in the aisle seat and Sarah in the window seat. Immediately in front of Wally's seat were the toilets – one on each side of the aisle – and then the flight deck. The flight left on time, in the early evening, and we all settled back for a pleasant three-hour journey. About two hours into the flight the pilot announced that we had just flown over Barcelona and were on time. Just after this, there seemed to be a slight change in the noise of the engines and, looking out of the window, I could see that the propeller on the engine nearest to our seats had stopped.

The pilot attempted to start it but, after one or two ineffective turns, it came to a stop again. He tried once more to start the engine. There was a tremendous explosion and, at the same moment, the propeller tore through the side of the plane, through the nearest toilet cubicle and across the aisle to the opposite cubicle, where it came to rest. Mercifully, both cubicles were vacant at the time.

The cabin filled with what appeared to be smoke and the pilot put the plane into a vertical nosedive. I learned later that we had been flying at 28,000 feet and he had nosedived to 10,000 feet to save irreparable damage to our eardrums – and what we had thought was smoke was in fact cloud, through which we were diving. At the time, however, we all assumed that the plane was on fire and was crashing into the sea. Now that the cabin was open to the elements and the roar of the remaining three engines, there was no possibility of my speaking to Wally or any chance of announcements by the air hostesses being heard.

I remember being extraordinarily calm. I removed the girls' shoes, loosened the collars on their dresses, took the lifejackets from beneath their seats and placed them over their heads, and shouted into their ears that when the plane reached the water I was going to push them out and they must try to hold on to any bit of plane they could. I think there is a strong element of Peter Pan in me: 'Dying will be an awfully big adventure.' After about ten minutes we realised that the plane was no longer nosediving and immediate immersion into the sea seemed less likely. The stewardesses made their way along the cabin, yelling loudly to each of us that we were turning back to Barcelona and, indeed, within twenty minutes we made our descent.

It was quite a dramatic arrival. There were water cannons ranged along the runway and, as soon as the plane came to a standstill, we were ordered to vacate it immediately and leave all personal possessions – bags, coats and, in our case, the children's shoes – behind. We were hustled into a waiting coach and driven to the terminal while a team of safety experts examined the plane. It was quite an anti-climax to then be driven back to the plane, after it had been declared safe, to gather all our belongings and then to collect our cases from the baggage carousel in the terminal.

However, for me the worst aspect of the whole incident was then to have to go through Spanish Customs. Thirty minutes earlier I had been preparing to meet my Maker – now I found myself confronted by a Spanish Customs officer demanding that I open my case for inspection.

The children were getting tired and cross, and I was both angry and indignant, especially as my command of the Spanish language was hopelessly inadequate to express my feelings. However, it seemed that it would be best to comply with his demands and get into the main terminal as quickly as possible. When eventually we emerged into the terminal we were given a meal of chicken and chips – although by this time I felt that a few double brandies would have been more appreciated! We were then told that the crew of a British United plane, which had landed just after our plane, were prepared to fly us on to Majorca that night. Of the seventy passengers on board, sixty-eight of us took up this generous offer and, five hours later than scheduled, we finally reached our hotel.

Some months ago, when a similar incident occurred, it warranted considerable television and radio news coverage – interviews with numerous passengers and of course the ubiquitous 'counselling' offered. Our incident was reported in a two-inch, single-column article in our local paper five days after the event!

In hindsight, perhaps counselling would have been a sensible option for, although we passed the whole matter off very lightly at the time, three days later the full significance of it seemed to hit Wally and he began to think of the return journey home with trepidation. He viewed the incident as being an omen – a warning against travel by air. I, the eternal optimist, felt that we could fly a million miles before anything like that would happen again. Many years later, and upon reflection, I think that he was probably right. It was an omen – not merely against air travel but against travel by any method you care to name: boat, train, car, donkey. In fact, it was probably a warning that we should avoid travelling further than the bottom of our own back garden. But this is being wise after the – many – events.

Chapter 2

1967/68 – To Palma (again) and Bigbury-on-Sea

The arrival of our son in 1965 and the move to our new house in 1966 put holidays out of the question for those two years. However, we decided to go back to our favourite holiday hotel in Majorca in 1967 – again flying from our local airport. The journey went smoothly but it was obvious that Wally was far from happy. In fact, he spent the next few mornings trekking into Palma to visit various travel agents seeking alternative travel for our return journey. On the fourth day he returned triumphant. He had found out that we could take a twenty-four-hour boat journey from Palma to Barcelona and then a succession of trains to Calais, a further ferry trip from Calais to Dover, and a further two train journeys to get home. I told him he was most welcome to do so, but I would be returning with the four children by plane. Reluctantly he gave in and we all returned together, but it was accepted that this was probably the last time we would fly as a family. In retrospect, that proposed journey by boat and train seems almost idyllic in comparison with the journeys that lay ahead of us.

In late 1967 our family increased further with the addition of our two foster daughters, Angela, then fourteen, and Teresa, aged ten. It did not require a financial genius to calculate that a flight-based package holiday abroad for eight on our income was simply not going to be feasible. Thus in 1968 we decided to explore the possibilities of self-catering holidays in the south-west of England. Of course, being completely naïve, we failed to realise that holiday homes large enough to house a family of our size – with a beach within easy walking distance – were fully booked years in advance during the school holidays. In our case there was simply no room to manoeuvre on dates, as Angela had end-of-year exams to complete and her school sports day to attend, and I was expecting our fifth child during the first week of August. We had almost abandoned any hope of finding a suitable property when a friend told me of a bungalow in Bigbury-on-Sea in Devon and, upon telephoning the owner, I found that it was indeed free for the two weeks required.

Having spent our last three holidays in Majorca, we were unprepared for the impact that the uncertainties of the British weather could have on a beach holiday with six children. We were due to leave on the Saturday but, two days before, Devon suffered torrential rain with severe flooding and the prospect of having all six cooped up in a bungalow in a small and possibly water-logged village was daunting. At least in our home town there was an abundance of cinemas which, being the school holidays, were showing a variety of films of appeal to children This, you will appreciate, was some fifteen years before the advent of videos. Also, at home they were able to visit friends or have friends round to play and while no doubt the proximity of the beach would, under normal circumstances, more than compensate, it was not going to do so in persistent rain. I telephoned the owner of the bungalow, who confirmed that the rain was very heavy and showing little sign of stopping. I telephoned again the next morning only to be told that there had been no change in the weather. On Monday I once again received the same reply, but on Tuesday – oh joy – I was assured that the sky was blue, the sun was out and the sea was sparkling.

We wasted no time in gathering all the cases and boxes which had been stacked in the hall and loading them into the cars. We had already decided that we would have to take two cars, so with Teresa, Jane and Sarah in Wally's car, I took Katie, John and our mother's help, Barbara, in mine, along with Timmy our Shetland sheepdog.

It had already been decided that Wally would come back for Angela after her exams and sports day and bring her to Bigbury on the Friday. The journey itself went well enough. The M4 and the Severn Bridge were both relatively new, and we bowled along quite happily before turning off on to the A38 heading to the south-west.

We eventually reached Bigbury-on-Sea and were relieved to find that the bungalow was indeed very near the beach. We naturally discovered some interesting little foibles about it – for example, the inside of the bath had been painted to cover the ravages of time and previous tenants. It looked very nice, but unfortunately coated the user with tiny flakes of white paint which were almost impossible to remove. The problem was eventually overcome by lining the bath with three towels before filling with water. This proved quite successful but caused a severe shortage of towels both for the beach and for post-bath drying.

We enjoyed Wednesday on the beach but Thursday was marred by the arrival of yet more rain. On Friday, Wally drove back home to Cardiff to collect Angela and by Friday evening the family was complete and ready to start the holiday in earnest. On Saturday we were all settled contentedly on the beach when Jane, then aged eight, had a major convulsion and fell unconscious on the beach. Jane had been born with hydrocephalus but an operation at the age of three had enabled her to live a completely normal life with only very occasional mild fits. So, faced with her lying on the beach unconscious, we were frantic and I raced to the public phone box and rang her paediatric specialist at his home. He was wonderful and told me to drive her straight away to Plymouth General Hospital and he would phone them and explain her condition to them. Leaving Barbara to cope with the remainder of the family, Wally drove straight to Plymouth while I sat in the back of the car with the unconscious Jane stretched across me.

It is only seventeen miles from Bigbury to Plymouth but the narrowness of the roads and their many twists and turns ensured that it took us an hour and a half to cover the distance. As our car rolled through the hospital gates, some vital part fell off and it refused to move another inch. I left Wally to deal with the car and followed my stretcher-borne daughter to the children's ward where they were waiting for her. Wally found a mechanic to fix the car, and then felt that he should return to the rest of the family, and so I settled down for an all- night vigil beside Jane's bed. Her condition, it transpired, was caused by nothing more than a severe ear infection, which was immediately treated with antibiotics. She recovered consciousness at 2 a.m. and, when offered a cup of tea, added that she would also like a biscuit. At this point I felt I could take myself off to the bed which had been provided for me, and soon fell asleep.

Wally returned the next morning and we were greatly relieved to find that Jane had fully recovered and was happily playing on the ward with the other children. We stayed with her for a while but it was obvious that we could not compete for her attention against her newfound friends and the collection of toys on offer, so we went out for lunch and, after an hour or so spent on the ward with her, returned to Bigbury. The next morning we set off again to visit Jane and talk to the paediatrician. He told us that he was satisfied with her and we could take her home the next day, so back we went to Bigbury hoping to enjoy a few hours of sunshine on the beach. When we arrived, Barbara told us that John had slipped on the wet grass playing football, and seemed unable to move. Various attempts on our part to stand him on his feet and get him to walk were of no avail, and there seemed no alternative other than to put him in the car and repeat the journey to Plymouth General Hospital.

We took him straight to A & E where an X-ray revealed that he had broken a bone in his leg, which had to be put in plaster. We were also told that he had to return in two days to have the plaster checked. We called in on Jane and told the staff what had happened. The next day (Tuesday) we set off to collect Jane and bring her back to Bigbury, and the following morning found us travelling that well-worn route to take John back to have his plaster checked. Just as we were leaving, a formidable sister from the maternity ward swooped on me and suggested that I attend their antenatal clinic that afternoon. I didn't stop to argue; I fled straight to the car lest I became the third member of our family to require the services of Plymouth General Hospital. We had two further days when the weather proved kind to us and we spent them on the beach. Everyone enjoyed themselves – apart from John, who was unable to go into the sea and found even walking on the sand a trial with his plaster.

Our journey home went smoothly and, as the winter set in, we began to think again of holidays. Although out of our original thirteen days of family beach holiday we had only managed three, it seemed unfair to place any blame on Bigbury. Devon does not flood every year, Jane could just as easily have developed an ear infection at home, and John likewise could have slipped in our own garden. However, had we been at home, we would have been two miles from one of the country's largest teaching hospitals – a five-minute car journey in each direction instead of a three-hour round trip.

Chapter 3

1969 – Port Isaac in Cornwall

For our next holiday we decided on Cornwall, and found a bungalow advertised as 'two minutes from the beach'. As the previous year, we set off in our two cars. By this time Barbara had left to get married and a young girl called Alison had taken her place. I took the younger members of the family and the dog with me. The journey was – by our standards – comparatively incident-free (discounting the fact that both the baby and the dog were violently sick in the car).

This merely confirmed my long-held belief that the effectiveness of travel-sickness pills lies in their psychological effect on their user and, unfortunately, neither eleven-month-old Brendan nor Timmy the dog understood that. Both incidents occurred as we were travelling along the section of the A38 known as Portway – the main road into Bristol and, prior to the construction of the M5 motorway, the only practical route to the south-west. Given the volume of traffic it is required to carry, it is a comparatively narrow road, bounded on one side by the towering face of the Avon Gorge and on the other side by the river Avon itself, and it affords absolutely no opportunity to pull off the road. I have always felt that stopping on that particular stretch of road would – if no longer a hanging offence – at least carry a heavy fine or a prison sentence. Since there was no question of stopping to clear up I pressed on, becoming increasingly aware, as I looked in my rear-view mirror, that the faces of the remainder of the party were becoming paler and even taking on a faint greenish tinge. It was more than thirty minutes before we were able to stop and improve travel conditions all round, and then we went on to Port Isaac.

Our journey ended at last outside the door of our bungalow, and we realised immediately that a certain amount of poetic license had been used in describing it as 'two minutes from beach.' There was indeed a shingle beach at the bottom of a very steep hill, but fishing boats took up most of the space and there were several signs warning that it was unsafe for swimming. Even an enthusiastic athlete would have had a problem making the return trip in less than ten minutes, and for a party of ten, including a toddler, a baby in a pushchair, carrying buckets, spades, rubber rings, swimming clothes, towels and enough drinks for a two-hour stay on the beach, it was impossible to manage it in less than half an hour. In fact, after our first excursion to this beach, we decided that it was not to be attempted again and, if we were to retain any semblance of holiday spirit, we would have to find a more satisfactory beach with suitable sand and safer sea for the children. Fortunately, one of our two cars was an estate and, by settling two children in the boot and sitting others on laps, we managed to get our entire family into it for our daily trip to the sands. (This, you will appreciate, was in the late 1960s when seatbelts were unknown – let alone compulsory.)

We discovered a beautiful spot twenty minutes drive away. Daymer Bay was an enormous expanse of sand with dunes stretching beyond it. The car park, however, was very small, holding no more than thirty cars, which ensured that the beach was never crowded. The lane leading to it was very narrow and winding and consequently, as soon as the car park was full, subsequent arrivals had to reverse a mile or so back up it. We were only caught out once in this way and after that would marshal the troops and their half-eaten breakfasts out of the bungalow and into the car, in order to make sure that we could get a place in the car park. There was something ironic about this as, when we had planned the holiday, we had seen it as a well-earned rest from the usual rush and scramble of our everyday lives. Now we had to rise and rush through breakfast even earlier than during term-time at home. At least at home we did not have to prepare ten packed lunches and load the car with buckets, spades, towels and other paraphernalia before we set out!

After we had booked our holiday we learned that our very good friends from the Midlands, Edna and Jim, were also intending to holiday in North Cornwall with their four children. However, they were planning a camping holiday as Jim, in a fit of totally misplaced confidence, had purchased a tent in which, he assured Edna, they would be able to spend many happy carefree holidays at minimum cost. Edna is a pragmatist and was considerably less optimistic.

We had arranged that, as soon as they arrived at the end of our first week, they would call over to Port Isaac and let us know where they were camping. So we were very pleased on our second Sunday to find, on our return from Daymer Bay, that they had left a note telling us that they were camping at Tintagel Head, only a short drive away. We decided to visit them early the next morning and join forces for a trip to the beach. Next morning we awoke to find rain pouring steadily down. We thought it imperative to find our friends and bring them and their children out of their tent and into the comparative comfort of our bungalow. Arriving at the camping site, we easily found them. Edna was standing inside the tent with just her arms and head poking out as she attempted to cook some bacon in a pan over a small stove. The expression on her face told us all we needed to know about her opinion of camping in general; and camping in the rain in particular. None of her family needed much persuasion to abandon the bacon and pile into their car and follow us back to Port Isaac, stopping on the way to stock up on pasties and chips for all.

The afternoon started quite peacefully – as peacefully as any afternoon can when eleven children are amusing themselves in a modestly-sized bungalow. The older children had settled in the dining room playing Monopoly or snakes and ladders (according to age and intellectual ability), and we parents took up positions in the small living room while our youngest offspring, both eleven months old, crawled around us.

We chatted in a desultory manner while watching whatever sporting offering was available on the 14-inch television when suddenly there was a slight creaking sound from the corner of the room where Jim was sitting in one of the two armchairs. The creaking sound rose to a crescendo, and Jim disappeared under a mound of white plaster which was followed rapidly by a stream of water. The torrential rain, proving too much for the bungalow roof, had brought down the ceiling. As he emerged from beneath the plaster he gave me a quizzical look and asked, 'How much are you paying for this bungalow?'

When we finally stopped laughing we dried him out and we all had tea – although Jim and Wally opted for a restorative beer. Admittedly the sitting room – not large to begin with – was now considerably reduced as the space previously occupied by the armchair was now filled with two large washing-up bowls, a bucket and an assortment of saucepans. Around 7 p.m., as our visitors prepared to leave, we noticed that, although the rain had stopped, the wind seemed to be rising and the waves out at sea were very much higher than earlier. It was evident that a storm was brewing.

We assured Ed and Jim that should they have any qualms about staying in their tent overnight they would be more than welcome to stay with us. Despite their protestations, Wally insisted that we make provision for their possible return during the night, and by doubling up our own children we managed to vacate one double and one single bed which, with the sofa in the living room, would be perfectly adequate for an emergency overnight stay.

We all went to bed early, prepared to be disturbed during the night by the intrepid campers who had been forced to take advantage of our offer, and consequently we were almost disappointed to wake in the morning to find the sun streaming in at our window and the sea as smooth as a millpond. Breakfast was completed in record time and we set off for the beach where – weather permitting – we had arranged to meet up with our friends. We were not altogether surprised when they failed to appear, suspecting that they had probably had very little sleep. However when we got back to our bungalow in the early evening all was explained. A telegram lay on the mat. It was marked 'Leominster 9 a.m.', and its message was terse. 'Tent blew away in the night. Gone home. Love Ed.'

Three weeks later, when we were back at home, Ed and Jim visited us and Edna gave us a full description of their night at Tintagel Head. After leaving us they had returned to the campsite. However, as the night wore on the gale increased and Edna, being a lady of caution and foresight, had suggested that they leave the tent and go into the car. This suggestion was scorned by Jim and the two elder children. However, Edna decided that discretion was the better part of valour and, taking the two younger children with her, settled them in the car. She was thus awarded a grandstand view of the scene which was to follow. The gale became fiercer and fiercer and finally, at about 2 a.m., one almighty gust lifted all the tents clear of their pegs and hurled them into the fields beyond. Edna, taking a totally detached view, was able to appreciate the scene of a hundred or so campers struggling out of sleeping bags, searching for footwear and desperately rushing around the site and clambering through hedges in pursuit of their property. One man in particular appealed to her sense of the ridiculous. He determinedly chased his tent across the adjoining field and, having rescued it, returned to his pitch and carefully (and after neatly folding it into a small package, much as when it had been purchased) walked over to the camp waste bin and deposited it firmly inside.

Jim and the two older children rescued their tent and their now broken tent pole, and, making no attempt whatsoever at methodical packing, piled the lot into the car and headed for home. Despite our disappointment at our friends' unexpected early departure, the holiday passed smoothly – although I am not sure that the older girls will ever forgive me for forcing them to join in the Floral Dance from Port Isaac to Port Gavin – a weekly tourist attraction at that time.

Our tenancy ended on the Friday morning and so we packed most of our belongings on Thursday night intending, should the morning be sunny, to have an early breakfast and spend a few hours on our favourite beach before beginning our homeward journey. Alternatively, if the weather was disappointing we would still leave early and have a leisurely drive home. It must be remembered that in the late 1960s, with plans for the M5 still on the drawing-board, the journey from Cornwall to Cardiff would normally take between eight and nine hours. (Note that in 1978 we completed this same journey in three and a half hours!)

If our journey down to Cornwall had been reasonably uneventful, the same could not be said of the return trip, and indeed the series of incidents on this journey determined the location of our holidays for years to come.

Chapter 4

1969 – From Cornwall to Cardiff

We woke early in the morning to be confronted by a mist which seemed unlikely to lift for several hours. Accordingly, we packed ourselves into our two cars and headed for home soon after 9.30 a.m. I realise that Devon and Cornwall are among the most popular holiday destinations in Britain, and I appreciate that the majority of holidaymakers interested in a beach-type holiday are restricted to the school holiday period. Nevertheless, I was totally unprepared for the wholesale migration of the British population which took place on that Friday in early August 1969. As we crawled along at 15 miles per hour it seemed to me that half the country were headed out of Cornwall, while the other half were headed in. By 5.30 p.m. we had covered one hundred miles and were three miles west of Wellington in Somerset, on the notorious A38 with two lines of cars in each direction travelling bumper to bumper. On our way we had seen numerous cars pulled off the road onto the grass verge with bonnets lifted and worried-looking families gazing in consternation at their engines. A few seemed to have run out of petrol and we were quietly congratulating ourselves on having made certain that we would not be caught out like that – when the clutch on my car broke. We were at the top of a small incline and, with great presence of mind, I urged Sarah to get out of the car and run to her father, three or four cars ahead of us, and tell him to take the next turning left – wherever it was heading.

Very fortunately, there was a left turning into a country lane fifty yards ahead and, being on a downward slope, I was able to roll my car down and follow him into it. Wally set off at once to find a telephone box (there were no mobile phones in 1969) and organise a rescue and I tried to be cheerful for the benefit of the family, but in this I was seriously hampered by Alison (who was a pleasant girl, but lacking in the pioneering spirit and prone to periods of depression). She sat by the roadside mentally wringing her hands and wailing, 'What shall we do? What shall we do?' Wally returned and reported that the AA had been alerted and promised to contact a local garage with a breakdown truck. By this time the others in the party were beginning to feel hungry. It was obvious that we were not going to find a welcome roadside cafe or farmhouse offering afternoon teas in this narrow country lane. I rummaged through both cars and discovered several biscuits of dubious age and origin, half a pot of marmalade and a bottle of tomato sauce. I defy any reputable chef to produce an appetising meal from those ingredients, and the expressions on the faces around me confirmed this.

I had just finished spreading the marmalade over the biscuits with the end of my pen when the breakdown truck turned into the lane. The biscuits were scattered to the ground in the excitement. Any relief which I may have felt on seeing it quickly vanished at the sight of the driver. Now, I know it is a sign of advancing age when policemen appear to be very young, but could the same apply to breakdown-truck drivers, for the youth who appeared at the wheel of this one looked barely old enough to be in secondary school, let alone hold a driving licence.

'Hop in yer car, missus,' he called out to me as he started to work a tow rope with surprising expertise. 'Now just steer it after me.' I have been towed on several other occasions. My memory of these is that we have proceeded at a steady – perhaps even funereal – pace. We have proceeded with dignity, caution and control, none of which could have been used to describe the manner in which I was towed by my adolescent rescuer. He seemed incapable of driving at less than 50 miles per hour or of taking a corner on more than two wheels. I must confess to actually shutting my eyes during some moments on the journey – especially the part where he took us straight across all four lanes of traffic on the A38 at breakneck speed. I know that, left to myself to nose my way across, we would still have been there at midnight. Wally – not a speed merchant – nevertheless threw caution to the wind and followed hard behind us, aware that if he lost contact with us he would have no idea where we had gone. I can only assume that the other motorists – all four lanes of them – were blessed with a sense of self-preservation and halted just prior to his dash across the road, leaving a clear right of way.

At last we drew up outside a garage in Wellington. We had already decided that Wally would remain with my car, while I took the family home in his. He began to transfer the more essential luggage from my car into his Vauxhall Cresta. This car was, by most standards, a roomy enough vehicle. Nevertheless, when loaded with several cases, it was asking a lot to then pack in two adults, two teenagers, four younger children, one baby and a Shetland sheepdog. However, we were at last crammed in and Wally bade us farewell and set off in search of whatever hotel comforts Wellington might have to offer, calling out cheerfully, 'Drive carefully! See you at home tomorrow.'

As I turned the car back towards the now dreaded A38 I felt a pang of envy as I compared his prospective evening – a good dinner, a few drinks and a pleasant hotel – with what undoubtedly lay ahead of me. The traffic on the A38 was still extremely heavy and between 7.30 p.m. and 8.30 p.m. we travelled exactly five miles. At this rate, I calculated that it would take us seventeen hours to reach home. However, there were a few isolated stretches where it was possible to increase our speed to 20 mph and occasionally even up to 30 mph. Our spirits rose as home became less of a mirage and more of a reality. This did not last for long, however, as the Cresta began to backfire in a most alarming manner. I pulled up at the next garage. 'Nothing to worry about,' diagnosed the friendly and optimistic attendant. 'Stop for a while and it'll soon cool down.' Seeing a roadside cafe a little further along, I jerked towards it and parked outside.

A salubrious establishment it was not. The clientele were mainly motorcyclists – all male and clad from head to toe in black leather. Our party, composed mainly of females, attracted a certain amount of comment – not all complimentary. However, ignoring all remarks I settled the children at two tables and, taking Alison and Angela with me, went to the serving counter. From an extremely limited menu, I selected bacon, eggs and chips as being most likely to prove popular with our group. Chips were unfortunately 'off', so we settled for bacon and eggs for eight and a few biscuits for baby Brendan.

Once the food was served, I sent Alison and Angela back to our tables while I paid the cashier and went to collect the cutlery. There appeared to be a total absence of either forks or spoons so I asked the somewhat harassed counter assistant where I might find some forks. 'All out the back – want washing – haven't got time' was her reply. Rather dashed, I made my way back to our tables. 'There aren't any forks,' I began brightly, 'so we'll all have to eat with our fingers.' In normal circumstances at home I feel confident that this would have been greeted with exclamations of delight and a desire to experiment at once with this rather novel way of eating bacon and eggs, and I was therefore quite unprepared to hear Sarah, then aged eight, say in a clear and carrying tone and painfully refined accent, 'I think it is ridiculous to expect people to eat bacon and eggs with their fingers.' I implored her to be quiet and eat up, but she was not to be deterred. 'But I do think it's ridiculous and very messy too.' On this last point, I agreed with her. Then Katie and John joined in with loud demands for forks – I think they had either burned their fingers on the bacon or found that fried eggs have a tendency to slip from little fingers.

All eyes were turned towards our tables. In desperation I returned to the serving counter. 'Please can you get me some forks?' I begged. With ill-concealed temper, the assistant flung a collection of wet forks at me. 'You'll have to dry them yourself – I haven't got time to fuss.' By this time I was too tired and embarrassed to argue, so controlling my temper, and realising that any further discussion on the matter would only create a scene and attract even more attention, I picked up the forks and set about drying them on my T-shirt – there also being a total absence of paper napkins.

The children were hustled as quickly as possible through their meal and we returned to the car. 'No more trouble now,' I said, clinging to the encouragement given by the garage assistant from earlier. I suspect that his knowledge of car mechanics was roughly equal to mine, for the moment I started the engine the car backfired with an ear-shattering blast and heaved itself forward with a violent jerk. We continued in this fashion for a further six or seven miles until at last we reached the town of Bridgewater. We were greeted with acclaim by crowds of teenagers who were attracted by the noise that heralded our approach. Loud cheers mingled with some rude remarks marked our progress along the main street. Our first attempts to find a garage advertised in my AA handbook as offering night service proved abortive, and my effort to cope with the one-way system, together with the very audible accompaniments from the car, soon brought us to the attention of two police constables, one of whom had unfounded pretensions as a motor mechanic and made a cursory attempt to diagnose the problem. The other, with greater wisdom, directed me to a garage which he thought may be able to help if it were not closed. It was open, and the mechanic declared that we had a major problem, and suggested we stay overnight in the town with a view to having the car repaired the following morning. As it was by now past 10 p.m., I endorsed this suggestion wholeheartedly.

Reaching once more for my AA handbook, I quickly located the names of several hotels in the town. A short drive brought us to the door of the most highly recommended. I went to reception and confidently requested accommodation for nine. The receptionist could barely conceal her scorn at such audacity. 'We've been fully booked up since Christmas,' she informed me in a rather superior manner. I greeted this information with obvious scepticism – the idea that the town of Bridgewater should be such a popular resort as to vie with the coastal resorts further west seemed unlikely. She expanded a little on the subject, pointing out that many people making the long trek from the North or Midlands would break their journey here and, consequently, Friday and Saturday nights were booked months ahead. Of course: how obvious, how ridiculous, how terrible for us. I explained our predicament and, in fairness, her hitherto supercilious attitude changed and she telephoned several other hotels in the town. One of these had two rooms available, so, thanking her profusely, I raced back to the car and headed in the direction given. I am afraid that I failed to follow these directions as well as I might have, because the journey of less than a mile took twenty minutes.

If the hotel, viewed from the outside, left much to be desired , inside it could only be described as seedy. Nevertheless, at that moment in my eyes it ranked with any five-star hotel you may care to mention. Unfortunately, it was not for us. The receptionist, in between picking her teeth with her elongated and purple-painted nails, laconically informed me that the two rooms had just been let as we had taken so long getting there. As I returned to the car to break this news to the family, the skies, which had been hinting at and, more latterly, threatening with rain, finally opened and released a veritable deluge.

If driving had been difficult before, it now took on a nightmarish quality. Alison consoled herself with another bout of wailing, 'What shall we do? What shall we do?'

'We shall drive out of the town a little and stop at a bed and breakfast place!' I said firmly as we clattered off. The first few places that we passed bore rather depressing 'No Vacancies' signs, but at last we came to a house set fifty yards or so off the road and there, hanging from a tree near the front gate, was a 'Vacancies' sign. My initial thought was to reverse the car up the drive, but unfortunately the turning angle was acute and I merely succeeded in reversing into a ditch. Leaving the car in this position, I leaped out and started up the driveway. This, I soon discovered, was severely scarred with potholes, several of which seemed to be two or three inches deep. The water in them lapped over my sandals and up to my ankles. I reached the front door and a charming man opened it. 'I'm so very sorry,' he replied to my request for accommodation, 'but we are full.'

'But your sign says 'Vacancies',' I pleaded.

'Yes, indeed it does,' replied the man, who was rapidly losing his charm. 'It's raining too hard for me to go down the drive and reverse it.' I turned and prepared to wade back downstream.

'I say,' he called, 'do you think you could just reverse the sign as you pass?'

I was dumbstruck – then, sparing a thought for fellow travellers who might well be misguided by it – my better nature came to the fore and I prepared to tackle the sign. However, I discovered that it was in fact some ten feet up and my philanthropy only goes so far and certainly does not extend to clambering up a tree in total darkness and torrential rain. Also, at this stage I had quite enough problems of my own to solve, the most immediate of which was releasing the car from the ditch. After a few minutes ferreting around in the hedge, I found a large stone and jammed it under the back wheel. Squelching back to the driving seat I turned on the engine and revved up and finally – giving its most heart-rending jerk of the evening – the car shot forward.

We clattered slowly along and I made a few more forays into those B&Bs still advertising vacancies. The reply was always the same: 'So sorry – full up – too wet to go out to change the sign. Could you change it on your way out?' In the main I largely ignored these requests, except in one case where the sign was actually on the gate and I felt it would be churlish to ignore it. The car could now only manage a top speed of 15 mph and this was achieved with tremendous jerks and accompanied by loud backfiring. It was now past 11 p.m. and we were still some seventy-five miles from home. My initial reaction was to press on but two factors deterred me. First, I was aware that I was becoming increasingly tired and may fall asleep at the wheel. Second, I doubted whether the car in its present condition would be permitted on the motorway and onto the Severn Bridge crossing.

I tentatively suggested to my passengers that we might pull off the road and try to sleep in the car. Alison, ever pessimistic, expressed the fear that with so many of us in the car we might all suffocate. I offered the idea of opening a window but, given the torrents still pouring down, Angela observed that those passengers nearest the windows would get extremely wet. Being already soaked to the skin myself, I was not overly sympathetic with this objection. While considering the relative merits of soaking versus suffocation we continued to clatter along the A38 when suddenly, out of the rain and darkness, loomed a road sign which was to offer us salvation. It was a simple enough sign, and it read 'Highbridge/Burnham-On-Sea'. Tired as I was, it triggered a memory in my mind – the address of a cousin seen only at infrequent family gatherings, but to whom I sent a card every Christmas addressed to Highbridge Road, Burnham-on-Sea.

'Walter and Helen!' I yelled out in relief. 'They must live near here. I'm sure they'll help.' A sharp left turn found us rattling into Burnham-on-Sea. I saw a phone box outside a small general store and post office. With shaking hands I turned the pages of the local directory in the box. I dialled the number. I could hear the ringing tone. 'Please let them be there,' I prayed silently. At last a woman's voice answered. 'Is that you, Helen?' I blurted.

'No, it's Sheila' – Sheila, their daughter whom I had met once in her twenty-four years. My words came tumbling out as I began explaining who I was and why I was phoning at that time of night. 'I've got seven children, my mother's help and a Shetland sheepdog and we've broken down. Do you think we could stay overnight with you? Anywhere will do,' I implored. They say blood is thicker than water and indeed it proved so. With admirable efficiency she determined exactly where we were and told me to wait in the car. Within minutes she arrived in her own car and we followed her back to her parents' house. Helen had already made a large pot of tea and had warm milk and biscuits waiting for the children – even a bowl of water and a few scraps for Timmy the dog. And, far from bedding us down on the living-room floor, which was my suggestion, she offered a double bed for me and the youngest children and single and camp beds for the others.

The next morning, after an excellent breakfast, Walter guided me in my embarrassingly noisy car to a garage where the fault was quickly identified and rectified. Then, after an equally good lunch which they insisted on providing for us, we set off for home. Wally was already there and completely mystified by our absence. 'Did you have a good evening?' I asked him, ready to regale him with our tale of tribulation. However, I was the one to be regaled. It appeared that every hotel in Wellington was also full of travellers who had wisely booked months in advance, and after he had tramped the streets of the town for several hours, the owner of a pub took pity on him and allowed him to sleep on a bench in the bar after closing time. Wally is a tall man and the bench was both narrow and short. Upon reflection, I possibly had the better night

Chapter 5

1970 – En route to St Cere

It might be assumed that after a journey such as our return from Cornwall, any hankering for holidays would have been dispelled forever and, given a family less blessed (or cursed) with optimism, this could well have proved to be the case. However, working on the premise that if a journey of 196 miles from Port Isaac to Cardiff could be such an utter disaster and take thirty-three hours, surely a journey to Spain could not prove much worse and there would be the added compensation of warmth and sunshine. Also, we discovered, Spanish rentals compared most favourably with those for holiday homes in the UK.

So, plans were made to rent a large house in Playa de Aro on the Costa Brava and to travel down at our leisure. We would take the overnight ferry from Southampton to Le Havre – with cabins – and then drive four hundred miles to St Cere in the Dordogne where an excellent family hotel had been recommended to us, and finally complete our journey by driving three hundred and fifty miles through the Pyrenees and on into

Spain. We were advised by friends who had made a similar journey to stick to the small back roads through France as they were comparatively traffic-free. At that time, France did not have a full motorway network, and the main roads were usually very busy. We had decided that it would be impractical to take two cars to Spain and, as one of our cars was reaching the end of its viable life, we turned it in and purchased a twelve-seater minibus.

I doubt if any general has prepared a troop move with more thoroughness than that with which I prepared my family for this journey. Every contingency was thought of and catered for, and we could hardly have been better equipped for a crossing of the Sahara Desert or a journey through a Malaysian jungle. In retrospect I cannot imagine why I assumed that France, civilised France, noted for the excellence of its food, would not have available in every town the many items which I took for the journey.

My enthusiasm for self- sufficiency, coupled with hair-raising tales of prices in French cafes, inspired me to provide packed meals for all ten of us – commencing with afternoon tea to be eaten on our journey to Southampton and finishing with afternoon tea to be eaten forty-eight hours later somewhere close to the Spanish border. At the time, banana sandwiches were a great favourite with the children, but we quickly learned how badly banana sandwiches travel. Made several hours before departure, the first packet of them was produced in the minibus on our way to Southampton and they were greeted less than enthusiastically. By the third day even I could not bring myself to offer them and discreetly dropped the final batch into a roadside waste bin. However, between leaving our home and arriving at our house in Spain, so much was to happen that a few discarded sandwiches were of no consequence.

The journey to Southampton was unremarkable and we were all excited on boarding the ferry and finding our cabins. Alison was again joining us and she, Angela, Teresa, Jane and Sarah were to share one cabin with four berths (Jane and Sarah to double up), and Wally, Katie, John, Brendan and I were to take another four-berth cabin. The first indication of a less than smooth trip came when Jane, who suffered from mild epilepsy, asked me for her tablets. I had got her prescription for four weeks' supply, I had taken it to our local pharmacy, received all the tablets and placed them prominently on the kitchen table to ensure that we would not forget them. I broke into a cold sweat as I could see quite clearly in my mind's eye those tablets still sitting on the kitchen table. The immediate solution that occurred to me was to telephone my parents and ask them to take them to Southampton and put them on the early morning ferry while we would spend the day in Le Havre awaiting their arrival. I rushed frantically to the purser's office, only to be told that the ship-to-shore line had been cut ten minutes earlier, as soon as we had sailed.

Wally exercised supreme calm in what could have proved a very fraught situation. 'We'll find a doctor first thing in the morning and get him to prescribe for her,' he said reassuringly. However, he did not say who exactly was going to explain the situation to the doctor and I had more than a slight suspicion that this task was going to fall on me. We managed to get off the boat without too much trauma – I still savour the memory of Alison running alongside the minibus trying to get her shoes on her feet and her rollers out of her hair before jumping on board. She had completely misjudged how promptly we would have to leave the ferry, and the men directing the traffic would stand for no delay in our moving off.

After driving for two hours, we reached the small town of Sees. A request for 'le medicin, s'il vous plaît' got a reply with easily understood directions to the doctor's house. It was a delightful old house standing in the main street. I tugged the bell-pull and an elderly maid opened the door to reveal a spacious hall tiled in black and white. The windows at each end were of coloured glass and the effect was truly enchanting – it could well have been used as a set for a late nineteenth-century film. The maid nodded towards a carved, high-backed chair in the hall and I sat down, composing my speech for the forthcoming meeting with the doctor.

Many years before, I had achieved a reasonable A-level in French. However, nothing in appreciating the works of French authors such as Voltaire and Molière or the Romantic poets had prepared me for a conversation regarding epilepsy and the treatment thereof. At last the door opposite me opened and a woman came out. The doctor came to the door and beckoned for me to come into the consulting room. He was quite a young man – perhaps in his early thirties, short, with fair hair, rimless glasses and wearing an elegant suit in pearl grey. I began 'Parlez-vous anglais, monsieur?'

He shook his head. 'Non,' he replied in such a firm manner that I knew that no further approaches could usefully be made in English. I took a deep breath. 'Je ne parle pas le français bien, monsieur,' and over the next few minutes I managed, with many gestures of my arms and appropriate facial expressions, to explain our dilemma. He grasped the general outline but problems arose when we tried to determine exactly what tablets she was normally prescribed. It appeared that brand names differed between countries and the names I was giving him were totally meaningless. At last he reached for a large book on the shelf behind him. It was some kind of drug catalogue and index. He pushed it towards me and after a while I managed to find the drugs I required.

Next came the problem of the strength of the drugs. I did not have the faintest idea. For years I had merely collected the prescription and Jane had followed the instructions on the packets: 'one tablet twice a day' for both drugs. It seemed that, in order to prescribe correctly, he had to know the severity of her attacks. They were in fact quite mild and occurred infrequently. However, the doctor proceeded to act out several types of epileptic attacks – including one in which he lay prone on the floor jerking his arms and legs alarmingly. I responded by giving a demonstration of Jane's 'petit mal' attacks – looking rather vague and moving my lips speechlessly. 'Ah!' he cried in triumph and, reaching for his pad, he quickly scribbled out a prescription for me to take to the pharmacy, which I understood was just a few doors away.

In my halting French I asked him how much I owed him, but he waved me away with a smile and indicated that there would be no charge. Considering that I had taken up well over three-quarters of an hour of his time and that his pearl-grey suit must surely require a visit to the dry cleaner after his demonstration on the surgery floor, I felt that this was most generous of him, and I realised that my command of the French language was far too inadequate to properly express my thanks. However, once we were in Spain I wrote to him, aided by a French dictionary, and I hoped he understood how much I had appreciated his help.

Of course, this stop in Sees – including the wait in the surgery before I saw the doctor and the collection of the prescription from the pharmacy – meant that we were now running about one and a half hours late. Consequently, we did not make our planned roadside stop for lunch – instead I fed the family a warm and flattened package labelled 'Lunch Day 2' – for which they showed scant enthusiasm. We stopped once or twice for petrol and necessary visits to the toilet, but Wally was becoming increasingly anxious to press on and reach our hotel before dark. The banana sandwiches in the package marked 'Tea Day 2' were totally unrecognisable and only the hungriest and hardiest of the group ate any of them.

Pressing on with our journey, we spent an interesting hour or so in Brive. Brive is a delightful small town some fifty miles south of Limoges. It was also the most confusing of all the towns through which we passed. Our directions had seemed perfectly straightforward but, no matter how carefully we followed them, we could not find the road which would lead us to our destination of St Cere. We entered Brive in broad daylight but night had fallen by the time we finally found our way out. I carried on countless conversations in my progressively worsening French with garage mechanics, paper-sellers, antique dealers, fruit-stall owners and two different policemen, none of whom proved to be of any assistance whatsoever; probably because my pronunciation led them to believe I was speaking in SerboCroat or possibly Urdu.

It was well past 10 p.m. when we finally saw the sign for St Cere and shortly afterwards drew up outside our hotel – the Hotel de Paris et du Coq Arlequin. The owners, Monsieur and Madame Bizat, despite our appallingly late arrival, could not have been kinder and assured us that our meal was waiting. Depositing our cases into the two large family rooms we had reserved, we hastily washed hands and faces and brushed hair and made for the dining room. We fell upon the food, which more than lived up to expectations – an enormous tureen of home-made soup and delicious home-baked bread, followed by chicken or lamb with perfectly cooked locally grown vegetables. The meal ended with a splendid selection of fresh fruits – peaches, pears, oranges, grapes and plenty of freshly brewed coffee.

At last, all truly well fed, we headed for our bedrooms. The hotel was an old one and narrow stairs wound up to the first floor where, in a five-bedded room, the five older girls were to sleep. This room had a hand basin and a shower in one corner. Wally and I and the three younger children continued up to the second floor where, once the children were settled in their beds, I went into the adjoining bathroom and ran myself a bath. I had just lowered myself into it and had begun to luxuriate in its warm deep water and unwind after what had been a very tiring day, when I heard Wally talking to Jane.

Seconds later, he called through the bathroom door. 'I think you'd better go down and see what the trouble is – it seems they are having a spot of bother with a tap.' Muttering very uncharitable remarks about my entire family, I dragged myself

out of the bath, leaving the water in, in the hope I might soon be able to return to it. As we had kept our hand luggage to a minimum, I did not have any form of dressing-gown with me, so there was nothing I could
do but dry myself thoroughly and drag back on my shirt and trousers. Jane was waiting for me and together we made our way down the winding staircase to the floor below. I opened the door to the bedroom and was greeted by a truly amazing sight.

On the side of the room farthest from the shower unit, Alison, Teresa and Sarah sat huddled on a bed – all three in their nightclothes. Standing right next to the shower was Angela, clad in a small towel. Between them stretched an expanse of water which was steadily spreading across the polished wood floor. At first I failed to appreciate the problem, but even as I stood there a face flannel suddenly shot out across the room – followed by a continuous jet of water. Resignedly, Angela walked across the room, picked up the flannel and, with a practised hand, stuffed it back into what I could now see was a hole in the wall. 'The tap came off,' she said and held out a small chrome object. 'The flannel stays in for a bit,' she went on 'and then it shoots out.' Judging by the amount of water on the floor, it had done this many times. As if to prove her point, the flannel shot across the room again. Despite the problem I began to laugh, for it was the same situation that I had once seen in an old Laurel and Hardy film. However, as it was now approaching midnight I felt that I should take command of the situation. I marched downstairs to the dining room where a young girl was setting the tables for breakfast. As I had grown increasingly tired, so my French had grown progressively worse and, abandoning any attempt at explanation, I caught her by the hand and pulled her out of the dining room and up the stairs. We went into the bedroom and, as we did so, the face flannel was making yet another journey across the room. The girl threw up her hands and then looked more closely at the shower. 'Le robinet, le robinet!' she shrieked and ran from the room. Seconds later she returned, accompanied by the young man who had been our waiter that evening. At the sight of him, Alison and Teresa dived under the bedclothes and even Angela, the intrepid, stretched around to try to find an extra towel. In a voice a few tones lower than the girl's he repeated 'Le robinet, le robinet!' and they both disappeared. Shortly afterwards they returned, accompanied by Monsieur Bizat himself who, in some dismay, summed up the situation in two words: 'Le robinet'. Then, recovering his composure, he explained in his excellent English that, in order to refit the tap, it would be necessary to turn off the water supply for the entire hotel.

He went away to do this and I waited with the girls until he returned with a few appropriate plumbing tools and refitted the tap. He turned with a smile. 'Now it will be possible for the young ladies to shower,' he assured us. As it was by now 1 a.m., I felt that the ladies young and old had long passed any enthusiasm for showers, but I thanked him wholeheartedly and wound my way back up to my room. Yes, the bath water was now completely cold, and I fell into bed too exhausted to care.

Chapter 6

1970 – The loss in Lot

Despite the previous day's exertions, we were all up early the following morning and after a most enjoyable breakfast were ready to leave by 8 a.m. It says much for the Bizats that they wished us a happy holiday and assured us that they were looking forward to our overnight stay with them on our return journey.

Over the years I had got into the habit of filming our family holidays. However, I hasten to add, I cannot be accused of being a home-movie addict, boring friends and relations with endless footage of relentless blue skies, silver sands and surf-swept sea. On the contrary, my films are so abysmally bad that they are normally shown only to those who at least have a sporting chance of featuring in them. These selected viewers can ignore the endless seconds of light flashes and can spend happy moments guessing whose legs are on screen or whose unremarkable shoulders are now being shown. They are in the fortunate position of being able to fill in for themselves the one moment that I failed to capture on film – such as Sarah's one perfect dive of the day. having meticulously recorded her climb up the rocks to the topmost point, filmed her hands lifted high above her head and then moved seamlessly to a shot of the baby eating an ice-cream – because I had failed to wind the camera sufficiently to record the dive itself. (Note: there were no digital cameras or camera phones in 1970.)

It was obvious that the trip to Spain was going to make a very special film and I began to film it as we left our house in Cardiff. I still think it starts rather well – a few shots of our minibus being loaded and the members of the family trooping out of the house and clambering aboard the bus – albeit somewhat self-consciously. Unfortunately, by the time we reached Southampton the light was too poor to take any further film, and as our start from Le Havre the next morning had been made with indecent haste and followed by the various delays en route to St Cere, I had given little thought to adding to our film. However, now as we were travelling through the Lot region of France I felt that a few more shots of us taking our refreshment in some picturesque spot would be a valuable addition. This part of France is incredibly beautiful and the route we had chosen took us through some quite breathtaking scenery – everywhere was so green and fertile and even the small houses seemed to have grown from the soil itself. They were all decently aged and every one had vines growing across, forming a shaded area at the front or side of the house. Geraniums in hues of scarlet, magenta and brilliant pink grew in window boxes in front of every house, shop and cafe. While for the passengers this scenery was a joy, for the driver the journey was a far from undisputed pleasure, as the roads wound around with steep drops on one side making driving hazardous.

As we were travelling along a particularly tortuous stretch, five-year-old John – sulking a little from boredom – stretched out his leg and knocked the handle of the side door of the bus. It swung open but, fortunately, as I was sitting next to it, I grabbed it quickly and locked it very firmly – at the same time sending John to continue his sulking at the back of the bus. About a half an hour later we decided to stop for a break and began looking out for a suitable picnic spot. We found one which seemed ideal – soft grass to sit on, trees to shade us, space to park the bus, a large enough area for the children to have a bit of a run and, above all, magnificent views.

It was now about 10.30 a.m. and we all climbed gratefully out of the bus. After drinks had been poured and handed out, and apples and oranges duly eaten, the children ran around exploring the little wooded area close by, while the older members of our little party enjoyed stretching out on the grass. I busied myself taking a few more feet of film of this idyllic scene. However, as we still had a lot of miles to cover, we soon returned to the bus. I remained behind to film everyone clambering back into it, but the scene that followed two minutes later would have been infinitely more film-worthy and it is to my lasting regret that there was nobody present to record it for us.

Everyone was settled in their seats and Wally had pressed the starter when I gave a cry: 'Where's my bag?' Totally uninterested, the older children looked around their immediate area.

'It's not here, Mum.'

'Can't see it.'

'Have you left it outside?'

Wally turned off the engine. 'We can't go on until we have it,' he declared. Of this, I was only too well aware. My handbag contained £100 in French francs, £50 in Spanish pesetas, £20 in sterling, our travellers' cheques and all our passports. Wally took control of the situation. Getting out of the driving seat, he came around to the side door of the bus. 'Everybody out,' he called and one by one everyone clambered out. 'Now, everyone search every inch of this area,' he commanded, pointing to the spot in which we had picnicked, despite my protests that I had not taken my bag out of the bus. He, meanwhile, was busying himself by systematically removing everything from the bus: jackets, sweaters, books, maps, biscuits, bottles, cards, talcum powder, packed meals and indeed every other item which he could discover either on or under the seats. All to no avail: my handbag had disappeared. As we sat forlornly on the grass, the scenery appearing considerably less idyllic than it had a little earlier, a flash of inspiration came to me.

The incident with John and the door had been forgotten, but it now occurred to me that it was probably then, as we were driving round a bend with the camber of the road falling away from the side door as it flew open, that my handbag had fallen out. I put this theory to Wally and he agreed that it was feasible. 'When did it happen?' he asked.

'Well,' I replied, 'at least half an hour before we stopped, but not further back than Figeac.' Wally did a quick mental calculation. 'So it must be somewhere between twenty and forty miles back,' he concluded. Silently I nodded. 'Right,' he said, 'everyone back in the bus.' Back we all clambered, in very different spirits from those we had been enjoying just fifteen minutes earlier. Wally turned the bus round in the narrow road and we drove at a speed that left little opportunity for admiring the scenery for about twenty miles. One or two of the older children posed the question, 'What will we do if you don't find it?' but they were quickly silenced. 'We will find it,' I said in a tone that forbade any argument. 'We will all pray to St Anthony' (St Anthony is the saint accepted as being of great assistance to those who are seeking lost items). At least the silent praying to St Anthony prevented any further questions and also gave me an opportunity to prepare a suitable speech in French. 'I have lost my handbag. It has fallen from the car. It is white and gilt and large.'

When we had driven the first twenty miles back Wally gave instructions that we were to call out when we came to a part of the road which looked similar to the stretch in question.

Unfortunately, there were numerous stretches of road that looked the same and, at each of these, the older girls and I had to get out of the bus and walk along the side of the road searching the grass bank and ditch. Some of these stretches of winding road were a mile or more long, and the girls were always glad to see a clear straight stretch ahead of us.

I greeted these with mixed feelings, as most straight stretches of road led through a small town or village where it was left to me to seek out the local police station or general store and recite my little speech. 'J'ai perdu mon sac. Il est tombé de l'auto. Il est blanc et gilt et grand.' Accuracy in grammatical terms was immaterial given my pronunciation problems and the towns of Sanvensa, Ville Franche de Rouverque, Farou, Villeneuve and Loupier all enjoyed in turn the dubious pleasure of my increasingly agitated company and my appallingly accented French. Each vine-covered, geranium-fronted police station or shop failed miserably to offer salvation. 'Non, madame, ce n'est pas ici.'

At last we completed the forty-mile return journey and arrived at Figeac. Figeac is a large town with a number of amenities. At that time it was also a great centre for French rugby. On our journey through it much earlier that morning I clearly remembered seeing a very imposing building set in spacious grounds with a sign that read 'Gendarmerie'. In fact, at the time I had commented that it was probably a police academy. At this point it seemed to offer our last hope. Wally turned the minibus in through the impressive gates and I got out and made my way towards the entrance to the building. I climbed the small flight of stone steps to the main door. Once inside the building I was confronted by a large, ornately carved counter behind which sat two gendarmes wearing immaculate pale beige uniforms. I once more ran through my well-worn speech. Slowly the two shook their heads, then, just as I had reached my lowest ebb, a door on the left was flung open and a man strode across the room towards me.

He was also dressed in a pale beige uniform with the addition of numerous stripes on his sleeves, presumably denoting rank. He had a small moustache and a gun holstered at his side, and could well have featured in a Hollywood film. He fixed me with a severe stare. 'Un sac?' he queried. I nodded. 'Blanc et doré?' Again I could only nod. 'Et grand?' Speech returned 'Oui. Très grand,' I stammered. He stretched out his arm, clicked his fingers. 'Suivez-moi,' he ordered. Meekly I followed him out of the door, down the steps and across the grounds to an open jeep. He opened the door. I prepared to join him on the passenger side. A look of irritation crossed his face. 'Non,' he said sternly. 'Vous suivez dans votre voiture.' Regretfully I released my hold on the passenger door and returned to the minibus and the seven children. 'He says we must follow him,' I explained to Wally. 'I think he must know where it is.'

It was fortunate that we were following such a distinctive-looking vehicle, for left to ourselves to find the tiny police station in the inner city, we could well have been searching all day. However, we were there very quickly, although some of the streets through which we travelled were so narrow that the wing mirrors on the bus brushed against houses on both sides of us. I know that, had we not been so desperate to keep our escort in sight, Wally would never have attempted to drive down them. The jeep drew up in front of an inauspicious-looking building – only a small sign saying 'Police' gave any indication as to its function. Our escort leaped from his jeep and signalled to me to follow him into the building.

Once inside he fired a series of commands to the two local policemen – hatless, short-sleeved and obviously extremely discomfited by the presence of this superior officer. Nevertheless, one of them opened a drawer under the counter and took out my handbag – white, gilt and very large. My joy knew no bounds! I reached out for it but, 'Non, non, madame,' he said and indicated that I must now check the contents off a list he had prepared. At this juncture my officer friend barked a few further comments to the two policemen and left. It was now up to me to begin the painful process of checking off all the items in my bag. It was fortunate that this was a new handbag, bought expressly for the holiday, and had only been stocked the night before we left. Thus I was spared the embarrassment that would normally arise from a close scrutiny of my bag. The fluff-coated half-eaten sweets, the age-old receipts from local shops, the collection of broken pens, loose lipsticks without lids, combs that should have been washed months ago (or preferably binned), all safely back at home. How thorough the French police are – not content with merely noting 'make-up bag', they had listed every item in it: 'One eye shadow Revlon – ice-blue; one lipstick Elizabeth Arden – shocking pink; one lipstick Rimmel – sweet coral; one comb – small, green.' Then came the passports, each one listed with the full name of the owner and complete number and place of issue. Then on again: 'One handkerchief – white'. I had momentary regrets at its unironed condition – as I did when we came to the two tissues (used)'. At last we came to my wallet. Absolutely intact in every way – not a franc, a peseta or even a pound missing. My French was totally inadequate to cope with this situation. I can only hope my face expressed my appreciation. I prepared to leave, but no – not yet. My full name and home address had to be noted. Feeling certain that the spelling of my Welsh-named road would completely mystify the policeman dealing with me, I handed over my driving licence and indicated that he should copy it from there.

He began very painstakingly to do so. Finally he reached the word Cardiff. He stopped and lifted his head 'Cardiff, Pays de Galle?' he enquired.

I nodded. 'Oui, Cardiff, Pays de Galle,' I replied.

'Cardiff, le rugby?' he asked.

I nodded again.

'Cardiff, le Cardiff Arms Park?' he further queried.

I agreed, 'Cardiff, le Cardiff Arms Park.'

He threw his arms up in delight and called out to a group of
fellow policemen who were in an adjoining room. They all
crowded in, examined my driving licence, clutched both my
hands and talked over and over of 'Le Cardiff Arms Park et le
rugby' while patting me on the back. I replied to their questions
to the best of my ability and in my euphoria at being reunited
with my handbag and their general acclamation, I think,
although I cannot be certain, that I offered an open invitation to
them all to visit me the next time France played Wales in
Cardiff.

Rejoining the family in the minibus, we set off once more on
our journey. I realised that I had in no way properly expressed
my thanks to the Figeac police force, and made up my mind that
once we arrived in Spain I would write and thank them
properly. This I did, and enclosed a small reward which I asked
them to pass on to the actual finder or, otherwise, to a local
charity. I was truly amazed to receive the next Christmas a
small card from Monsieur et Madame Georges Fraysse et leurs
enfants. It bore the message, 'Dear Mrs. Receive of people who
has find your bag.' We exchanged cards at Christmas for several
years afterwards, and I hope they realised how truly grateful I
was.

M. & Mᵐᵉ GEORGES FRAYSSE
ET LEURS ENFANTS

Dear Mrs,

*Receve of people
what has find your bag)*

LOTISSEMENT DE MONTVIQUIER   46 · FIGEAC

Chapter 7

1970 – Onward to Spain

We passed our picnic spot at 3.30 p.m., precisely five hours after we had made our morning stop there. Wisely, no one remarked on this. Any question of stopping for meals was obviously not to be given any serious consideration. However, as the last of our pre-packed meals had been consigned to the roadside bin, I managed to persuade Wally to stop at one village long enough for me to buy some fruit and biscuits which we ate as we drove along. One of the main highlights of our journey was to have been crossing the Pyrenees. We had intended to stop on our way across and add this magnificent scenery to our film. Needless to say, by the time we crossed the Pyrenees, darkness had fallen and it was quite difficult to make out the road itself, let alone any part of the landscape beyond. We consoled ourselves with the thought that we would be able to see them on our return journey. As it happened, our journey was made early in the morning and the mist still lay heavily on the mountains, completely obscuring them from our view. The Pyrenees did not feature significantly in our holiday memories.

At last we reached the French–Spanish border. The traffic moved very slowly for several miles but by this time we didn't care. We knew that the agent for our villa, Senor Junca, would be at his office until 11 p.m., and we were only too aware that it would be well past midnight before we reached Playa de Aro and, despite our travel agent's warning to try to arrive before 11 p.m., we would have no alternative but to go to his home. The inland Spanish towns were in complete darkness as we drove through them. Even Gerona – a large town of industrial and commercial importance – had few street lamps and, despite it being a Saturday night, we did not see a soul on the streets.

Playa de Aro was about forty miles further on from Gerona. We drove through a few more small towns, all in darkness, and therefore we were totally unprepared for the sight that greeted us as we drove over the last small hill before reaching the town. One minute, we were in complete darkness; the next, we were driving through a wide street with brilliant overhead lighting, shops and cafes all open and throngs of people walking along both sides of the street, every bar packed, cars driving bumper to bumper in both directions, music blaring from every cafe and seemingly from every car. I stared at it in disbelief. Was this really the resort which, above all others, I had selected as being ideal for my family? To my fatigued eyes, it seemed to be a latter-day Sodom or Gomorrah. Nevertheless, like it or not, this is where we were to stay for the next three weeks, and the sooner we found the agent and our villa the better for us all.

In the – he hoped – unlikely event of our needing it, our travel agent had supplied us with a small map of the town and instructions on how we could find Senor Junca's home. We had to drive along the main road for a mile or so and then turn left into Calle Reine Isabella. To my surprise and relief, the bright lights ended as abruptly as they had begun. In fact, the brilliantly-lit street was perhaps less than half a mile long and the area after that was given over to residential housing and open fields. We found Calle Reine Isabella quite easily and drove down this pleasant residential street until we reached the number we required. It was a large detached house with seven or eight wide stone steps leading to the French doors in the front.

I left the family in the minibus and went up the steps to the entrance. As I reached the glass doors I could see the figure of a man stretched out on a sofa on the far side of the hall. Of course, I thought to myself, Senor Junca will have waited in the hall to hear us arrive and save us disturbing the rest of the household. Very gently, I tapped on the glass. The figure lay still. I tapped again – no movement. I then quietly turned the handle of the door, which obligingly swung open. 'Senor Junca,' I called softly. No movement, no reply. 'Senor Junca,' I called again, tiptoeing from the doorway towards the sleeping figure. 'Senor Junca! Senor Junca!' I got no further – a door to my right was thrust open and a small ferocious middle-aged woman clad in a full-length flannelette nightgown, her hair screwed up in curlers, rushed at me with her arms outstretched. 'Non, non, non, non, non!' she shouted at me, placing both her hands on my shoulders and pushing me backwards out of the door. I was too surprised to protest or even stand my ground and, the next thing, I knew I was outside the door and the key in the lock was being very firmly turned from the inside.

Not quite believing what had happened, I returned to the bus and told Wally of this rather unexpected welcome. 'You can't have got the right house,' was his immediate reaction. Handing him the paper with both address and directions on, I left him to wander around the nearby houses for a few minutes. He returned to the bus. 'This has to be the house,' he conceded, 'but perhaps we should ask someone.' There was a notable absence of persons to ask at 1 a.m. in Call Reine Isabella, but we remembered seeing a small cafe on the corner and drove back there. We did not see anyone in the cafe but in the forecourt a woman stood frying squid over an open fire – a curious occupation for that time of the morning.

We produced our paper with the name of Senor Junca and the address. She confirmed that we were correct, and so we went back to the pleasant detached house. This time I absolutely refused to attempt an entry on my own. The only logical explanation for the irate lady driving me from the hallway without allowing me to say a word, coupled with the fact that the man – presumably her husband – was sleeping in the hall, was that she suspected him of having an affair and I, blameless mother of a large family, was mistaken for his mistress. I longed to correct this slur on my character and felt that the appearance of my husband and possibly the seven children from the minibus would certainly remove any vestige of suspicion.

Wally and I approached the glass doors. As Wally lifted his hand to tap on the glass, the figure on the sofa suddenly rose up and, with his finger on his lips, tiptoed across the hall. I noted with interest that he was wearing a full-length nightshirt and a nightcap. Apart from in films set in the Dickensian era, I had never actually seen anyone dressed this way. He quietly unlocked the door and motioned for us to go back down the steps. He followed us out, carefully closing the door behind him. Once at the bottom of the steps he drew us around to the side of the house – presumably out of earshot of his good lady. In heavily accented English he asked, 'You want Senor Junca?' We nodded eagerly. 'He is sous-sol.' He was evidently French and his English was deserting him with the lateness of the hour and his apprehension over his domestic situation. 'He is there – gauche.' He pointed to the left of the house, where we could just make out a flight of steps leading down to a basement flat. We began our thanks but, looking fearfully around, he flapped his hands at us to hurry us away.

We left him to his plight and went down the stone steps. At the bottom there was a lighted window and beyond that a wooden door. We rang the doorbell and a voice called out something quite unintelligible in Spanish. A few seconds later, a small sturdy balding man appeared. 'Senor Junca?' I queried. He held out his hand. 'Senora Laing?' he asked in return. We began our apologies for our late arrival together with our explanation. Senor Junca, however, spoke no English and the prospect of trying to explain the convoluted story of my lost handbag at that hour of the morning in my inadequate Spanish was beyond me.

Senor Junca indicated that he would travel with us in the minibus and direct us to our villa. It was only as I ushered him into the bus that I registered the full effects of the day's travelling. A more sordid scene would be difficult to imagine. The floor of the bus was inches deep in discarded biscuit packets, sweet papers, tissues, comics, paper bags, plastic bags, disposable cups and empty bottles – all easily cleared given a sufficiently long stop and a large bag for the rubbish. Unfortunately, our schedule for that day had not offered such a time-consuming luxury. Senor Junca stared incredulously at the bus and its occupants. In addition to having had no time to clean the bus, we had had no opportunity to clean the children. He was a noble man. Metaphorically, if not physically, gritting his teeth, he boarded the bus and, with a few clear directions, guided us speedily to our villa. Once there, he spent some two or three minutes switching on the water heater and fridge before going back to his flat. Wally offered him a lift, but he, wise soul, opted to walk.

Chapter 8

1970 – Playo de Aro and home

The children and I woke late after a refreshingly long sleep.
Wally, however, despite the previous day's long and traumatic
journey, had already been out and found the local Catholic
church and times of Masses, it being Sunday. He had also
bought freshly baked croissants and crisp bread rolls still warm
from the oven and, ravenous as we were after our previous
day's frugal diet, we ate them all. We decided to go to Mass
straight away and as we walked along the main street I was
most relieved to find that in daylight it looked perfectly
charming and innocent – compared with the impression I had
gained the night before. Mass over, we headed back to our villa
and prepared for the beach.

Our travel agent – a small, privately-owned concern – had
assured us that our villa was one hundred and fifty yards from a
two-and-a-half-mile stretch of sandy beach, and one hundred
yards from the main shopping street. After our experience in
Cornwall I must confess to having been extremely sceptical

about the likely truth of these statements, so I was delighted to find that my reservations were totally unfounded and both the beach and main street were exactly as described. The villa itself was all we had hoped for: it had four good-sized bedrooms, three of which opened on to a balcony on two sides of the house. Furthermore, there was a large upstairs bathroom with full-sized bath, lavatory and wash-basin of gigantic proportions, all in deep plum-coloured porcelain, and a further smaller shower room with lavatory and wash-basin. Downstairs lay a well-equipped kitchen and a large living room with French doors on two sides leading on to a wide veranda – and there was even a tiny cloakroom. All in all, we were delighted with our accommodation.

The following day, being Monday, saw the arrival of our maid. Our accommodation booking had included four hours a day of maid service – Sundays excepted: 'Maid to cook midday meal and clear away.' At 10 a.m. prompt, Maria arrived. She was, I suppose, in her mid-thirties – a cheerful dark-haired woman who spoke not a word of English but whose capacity for work I never expect to see equalled. Every morning after clearing away the breakfast dishes, she stripped all ten beds and hung all twenty sheets out in the ever present sunshine to air and, once each week, she washed them all. No matter that Wally and I and the older girls had made our beds before she arrived, all were stripped and, when we returned from the beach at lunchtime, we could be sure of seeing all twenty sheets pegged out on the lines. Not content with hand-washing all these sheets once a week, Maria would eagerly seize upon any clothes that had been left lying around and wash them too – returning them perfectly ironed the next day. In addition to all this, she would sweep right through the house and then wash all the floors which, in typical Spanish style, were tiled both upstairs and downstairs.

On the first morning she had asked me what she should prepare for lunch. My inadequate Spanish – the outcome of two winters' of evening classes at our local high school – coupled with our rather impecunious financial situation, resulted in my selecting potato omelette – mainly because I knew the words and we had bought both eggs and potatoes.

As the holiday wore on my Spanish did not improve and we consumed a lot of Maria's omelettes. She cooked them superbly, but towards the end even the most addicted omelette eaters were losing their enthusiasm. We varied the omelettes with ham salads. I had brought half a dozen tins of ham from home together with other expensive items such as tea, coffee, tinned butter and biscuits. Fruit was cheap and all the family were great fruit-lovers –
particularly of the more exotic and expensive variety, such as peaches, grapes and melons. Here we were able to indulge ourselves to the full, as these were among the cheapest in the market and all of superb quality.

Anxious to establish a good relationship with Maria and not appear aloof, on her second morning I prepared a few appropriate sentences in Spanish. I realised that she was married so I asked her, 'Do you have any children?' She replied in a lengthy torrent of quickly spoken Spanish, the general gist of which was that she had fourteen children. When I heard this, my own seven children paled into insignificance and I resolved that we must do all we could to lighten her load. The most practical way seemed to be to have lunch at 1 p.m. and tell her that we would clear away afterwards – that way she would be able to leave at least forty-five minutes earlier than her agreed finishing time. I am not sure that this charitable act on my part was welcomed by the older girls, upon whom much of the burden of clearing away fell, and even Maria herself seemed reluctant to take up the offer. However, I insisted and eventually she accepted what she regarded as a strange whim on my part.

Two days before our holiday ended, Maria arrived a little late. 'My little boy has spots,' she explained in her rapid Spanish. 'I had to send for the doctor.'

'Is it serious?' I asked, anxious for the remaining thirteen children.

'No,' she replied. 'He says it is nothing to worry about.'

'How old is he?' I asked.

'Seven,' was her reply.

'Who is looking after him?' I continued.

'My eldest daughter,' Maria answered 'She is fourteen.'

I pressed on with my enquiries. 'What about your other children?' 'My other son, he is ten, he is staying with his cousin,' said Maria, preparing to clear the dishes.

'But what about all the others?' I persisted.

Maria looked at me blankly. 'What others?'

'Your other children—' I began and then stopped, as at the back of my mind a clear explanation was forming. Of course, when Maria replied to my question as to whether she had children, she must have said, 'I have a son of seven, another of ten, and a daughter of fourteen' – but I had translated this as fourteen children, rather than the three which actually constituted her family.

I thought back on the last three weeks of dishwashing, and debated momentarily whether to ask her to stay and clear away on our last two days, but no – I would let her retain her memories of me as a benevolent – if slightly eccentric – employer. I felt it would be too humiliating to tell her that I had misunderstood the size of her family, and I also kept this information from my own family. Let it be a lesson to me: 'A little knowledge is a dangerous thing.' Especially when it is poorly-learned Spanish.

In both Devon and Cornwall the toilet and bathroom facilities had left much to be desired, but here in the Villa Munoz both were well above our expectations. However, during the second week of our stay the lavatory chain in the smaller upstairs bathroom broke off. A brief investigation revealed that the cast-iron plate in the cistern had snapped in two and, after a few ineffectual attempts at repairing it, I was forced to accept that my normal all-purpose repair kit for such emergencies – a roll of sellotape – had not proved noticeably successful. 'I'll call in to Senor Junca this evening,' I said airily. That was before I had scanned my handy Spanish phrasebook and pocket-sized English/Spanish dictionary. An exhaustive search of both failed to produce a satisfactory equivalent for 'lavatory chain'.

Undaunted by this, I popped the offending chain into my handbag and strode off to Senor Junca's office, where he sat on a stool on the far side of his high counter. 'Senora Laing,' he greeted me as I went in. 'Senor Junca,' I replied. We shook hands. Then, from my handbag I produced the chain and laid it flat along the counter. Senor Junca stared at it for a considerable time. He viewed it from the left, he viewed it from the right. He even got off his stool and stood directly over it. He was clearly bewildered. Finally, realisation dawned on him. Taking the chain in his right hand, he lifted it upwards and outwards and dangled it from his fingers. Then with his left hand he grasped the handle of the chain and gave a sharp pull. 'Si?' he queried. 'Si, si, si,' I replied. Senor Junca broke into a wide smile. 'Mañana,' he promised me. Previous holidays in Majorca had prepared us for the true meaning of 'mañana'. Well may the dictionaries lull you into a sense of false security by translating it as 'tomorrow'. We had learned from bitter experience that in fact 'mañana' can mean any time between July and Christmas.

I was therefore totally unprepared for the arrival of our visitor at nine o'clock the following morning. Soon after our arrival we had established a simple and practical mode of dress. Bikinis or bathing trunks were to be worn at all times apart from during trips to the main street in the evenings. Consequently nine o'clock found Alison, Angela, Teresa and I all in our bikinis preparing to leave for the beach. The younger children had already gone on ahead with their father. Teresa and I were upstairs, Alison and Angela were in the living room. Angela called out, 'There's a man here.' I leaned over the top of the stairs. There was indeed a man there, albeit a rather young one –

aged eighteen to twenty, I estimated. He was extremely tall with deep blond hair. In his right hand he clutched a small black leather bag and in his left I recognised our lavatory chain. 'Do you speak English?' I asked him as I descended the stairs. A blank look greeted me. 'Parlez-vous français?' I tried. Again no response.

At nine o'clock in the morning, my Spanish had deserted me completely, so I merely beckoned him towards me. He looked terrified. He stood there, flanked by a bikini-clad Angela on his right and a bikini-clad Alison on his left; above him stood a barely-dressed Teresa, while an even stranger older woman silently beckoned him towards her.

As England expects each man to do his duty, so no doubt Spain has some similar motto appropriate for such occasions. Holding firmly to his bag and the chain, he began to climb the stairs, staring straight ahead to avoid eye contact with either Angela or Alison. I went ahead of him, beckoning and smiling in what I fondly imagined was a reassuring manner. He bore up bravely. Nevertheless, when I showed him into the bathroom his relief was all too evident. His shoulders relaxed; he released his grip on the bag and the chain. Then, as quickly as was decently possible, he closed the door on our smiling faces and shot the bolt. We thought it best to leave him to get on with the job on his own, so with a few calls of 'adios', we left for the beach.

At the start of our second week's holiday we were walking along the main street one evening when, sitting outside a cafe, we saw the very friends who had recommended our travel agent to us. As they had moved away from Cardiff and we had not seen them for several months, we were all unaware that we had selected both the same resort and same weeks for our holidays. They told us they were celebrating their tenth wedding anniversary that week, and suggested that we might join them for dinner to mark the occasion. The four of us had a splendid evening consuming excellent food and copious amounts of local wine. We finished off the evening by calling at two or three small cafes for coffee and brandies, finally arriving at our villa in the early hours of the morning. It was a very civilised and adult evening.

A few days later, it was time to begin our trek home. We had reserved rooms at the same hotel in St Cere, and the Bizats made us most welcome – which was extremely generous of them considering the disruption we had caused on our earlier visit. Our friends with whom we had shared the anniversary meal were making the same stop so we were able to enjoy another very civilised meal together once the children – both ours and theirs – had been fed and dispatched to bed. We had one more night in France as we had decided to break the journey at L'Aigle in the north of France before taking the daytime ferry back to Southampton.

The Hotel Dauphin, which had been recommended by our travel agent, occupied the whole of one side of the small town square. It was four storeys high and four hundred years old. From reception a porter produced keys and prepared to lead us to our two family rooms. We asked to be taken first to the girls' room. As we mounted flight after flight of narrow stairs I became quite concerned, wondering what kind of garret was awaiting us. We were now right under the roof itself, as we could see from the exposed beams. At last the porter stopped. He placed the key in the door in front of him and turned the handle. What a fantastic surprise we had when we entered the room. it was beautifully carpeted with two king-sized double beds and a single four-poster bed, all with matching curtains and bedspreads in glazed cotton featuring a hunting scene which picked out to perfection the colour of the carpet. The walls were hung with a pale green silk. There were two armchairs and a small, low, marble-topped table and a further table at dining height and four dining type chairs around it. The room was so large that it did not seem in the least over-furnished. Beyond the bedroom lay a dressing room and the bathroom, all furnished throughout in the same matching tones. Very reluctantly we left the girls there to play cards, have a bath, wash their hair and generally enjoy their surroundings. We followed the porter back down two flights of stairs to our room. This was much smaller but equally attractive and we all spent a very comfortable night.

We left early the next morning and made our way to Le Havre and the boat home. We eventually arrived home at 11 p.m. As our car rolled down our drive I began to sing 'You Did It', a song from *My Fair Lady*: 'I say, old man, you did it, you did it, you did it.'

'Yes,' said Wally, 'but I never will again.'

Chapter 9

1971 – Playo de Aro (again)

Despite Wally's initial reaction to the prospect of undertaking a similar trip the following year, we had not been home for long before the trials of the journey faded and, faced with the cold Welsh rain, we remembered the sunshine, warm sea and gaiety of Playa de Aro. We decided that, as we now knew the town and had been very satisfied with the Villa Munoz, we should rebook for the following summer without further delay. Wally set about planning our route – this time very conscious of the strain of driving the minibus for long periods, as it was heavier to handle than a car and the driving seat offered no change of angle. We decided that we would take the day ferry to Le Havre – due in at 7 p.m. – and then drive to L'Aigle, staying overnight at the Hotel Dauphin once again before carrying on to St Cere. We wrote to both hotels and, to my great surprise, the Bizats accepted our booking and even added that they were looking forward to our visit.

By the summer of 1971, Alison had left us to get married and so we decided to take Julia, a school friend of Angela, in her place. So once again we set off in July: Wally and I, Angela, Julia, Teresa, Jane, Sarah, Katie, John and youngest son Brendan, who was now almost three. The boat journey was uneventful; however, I had forgotten that Continental time is one hour ahead of British time and in fact we arrived at Le Havre at 8 p.m. Furthermore, whereas the previous year we had been fortunate to be among the first to leave the boat, this time our minibus had been positioned in such a way that we were one of the last to leave.

These two factors meant that we arrived at L'Aigle over two hours later than we had planned, leaving us with no time to enjoy any of the room facilities or, for that matter, the restaurant food. In fact, by the time we arrived, we were all too tired to do more than fall into our beds and sleep soundly through the night.

The next morning we left at 7 a.m., not stopping for breakfast at the hotel, but intending to stop after a couple of hours for rolls, croissants and coffee. Once again however, fate conspired against us. This time the villain of the piece was a road improvement scheme taking place around a town called Nogent le Rotrou, a little way south of L'Aigle. Following the very explicit directions sent by our travel agent we arrived quite easily at Nogent le Rotrou. However, when we attempted to leave by our recommended route we found that we were being diverted to a different road. Not unduly bothered by this, we followed all the temporary signs for twenty minutes or so, leaving town buildings behind and driving through pleasant open country. Seeing a town ahead of us, Wally called to me, 'What should this place be?' I hauled out our map and consulted it. I was a little surprised that we had reached the next town so quickly as, looking at the distance on the map, I thought it would have taken us at least a further ten minutes to get there. However, as we reached the outskirts of the town we were totally disconcerted to read the sign 'Nogent le Rotrou'. We had obviously completed a part circle of the town by means of a devious country route and were now back where we had started! 'Now, let's get it right this time,' said Wally, so I clambered into the front seat of the bus in order to follow the road signs better – leaving Wally to concentrate on driving. We soon arrived at our original diversion and once again set off, carefully following all the signs.

This time we decided to make our turn southwards where four roads converged and drove on quite confidently for a further half an hour. The next town loomed up and, not being absolutely certain that we were on the recommended road, Wally said, 'See what this town is and check our position on the map.' I leaned forward and strained my eyes to try and make out the name. 'It can't be,' I said to myself, shutting my eyes for a few seconds. I opened them – we were nearer now and the sign was clearer. 'Well, what is it?' asked Wally, growing a little impatient and concentrating on the oncoming traffic. I blinked several times. 'Don't miss it!' shouted Wally as we drew level with the sign. He need not have worried, as the name was now fixed permanently in my mind. For a few moments I contemplated abandoning Spain entirely and settling for two weeks in Nogent le Rotrou. 'You're not going to believe this, dear,' I began, trying to keep a light and steady note in my voice, 'but it's Nogent le Rotrou.'

After a lengthy consultation of the map and a fragmented conversation with the men working on the road in my abysmal French, we eventually managed to reach our recommended route. Breakfast by now had long become a lost cause and even lunch was a hastily eaten affair of fruit and rolls by the roadside. However, we managed to reach St Cere in the early evening with an opportunity to explore the town before dark. It is a picturesque market town with a small stream running through it, upon which several swans were swimming. The children, however, opted to take a walk around the local graveyard,

which they had noticed as we had driven into the town. They had seen a number of French
graveyards both on our current journey and the previous year and had developed a fascination for them. Thus we spent an hour wandering among the graves looking with great interest at the small 'houses' which marked some family crypts, and also at some of the extremely ornate monuments on others. It may seem a slightly macabre way of passing the time, but both the children's interest and curiosity were more than satisfied.

We all enjoyed an excellent dinner at the Hotel de Paris et du Coq Arlequin and had plenty of time to savour it. Once again we had two family rooms, but this time the girls had a room with a self-contained shower unit – wise Monsieur Bizat.

Our next day's journey was uneventful – in sharp contrast to the previous year's – and we actually arrived in Playa de Aro before dark. Everything was as we expected. We went to Senor Junca's office and he came with us to the villa and explained that our maid would arrive on Monday morning. Maria was not available this year, but a new maid had been engaged for us.

On Monday morning at half past nine sharp, our maid arrived. She was rather older than Maria and seemed a little dour. She told us her name was Bencita and that she would cook a meal for us each day at lunchtime. What Bencita lacked in social graces she more than made up for with her cooking. She was an excellent cook and rather scornful of my limited choice of food. A further winter of evening classes in Spanish had done little to improve my ability to extend our menu. After a few days she led me to understand that she would purchase all the food for our main meal of the day. This alarmed me, as I had already noted the price of meat in Spain. Bencita merely shook her head and waved her arms. 'Not from shops,' she said scornfully, 'from my uncle.' It seemed, from the few snatches of her long explanation that I could actually understand, that she grew a wide variety of vegetables and that her uncle kept chickens. Indeed, the eggs and chickens that she produced for us were remarkably cheap and if they had fallen off the Spanish equivalent of the back of a lorry. I felt that there was little I could, or indeed would wish to, do to change this.

The holiday went along smoothly until one afternoon. We were all on the beach. Jane was badgering me to go for a swim. The beach shelved quite sharply a few yards out and we had made it very clear to the children that they should swim out only when accompanied by an adult or Angela or Julia. As the sun was really very hot, I was quite glad to get up and set off with her for a swim. I thought I might take the younger ones in with me. 'Where are Sarah, Katie and John?' I asked her. ' They were playing with the lilo at the edge of the sea,' she said. 'Who else was with them?' I asked sharply. 'No one else,' she replied. I felt a wave of panic. We had stressed over and over that no lilos were to be taken to the sea unless with an adult. At this time Sarah was ten and a reasonably strong swimmer and Katie at eight could swim quite well in a pool, but John at six had barely learned to swim a width of our local pool.

I looked along the water's edge. There was no sign of either the lilo or the children. I turned and ran back to Wally. 'Quick!' I called to him. 'I can't find Sarah, Katie and John. And they've taken the lilo!' Leaving Angela to look after Brendan, Wally headed towards the sea.

'You go that way,' he called to me, pointing to the left. 'And you—' he turned to Julia and Teresa, 'go and check all the drinks and ice-cream stalls along the beach.' We separated. I walked along the edge of the water searching among the bathers splashing about in the sea. Reluctantly I began to extend my gaze further out to sea, but saw nothing but a few pedalos, two small yachts and several sailing dinghies; no lilos. Then far out on the horizon I spotted a lilo with – and here the panic really overcame me – only two heads rising above it. I was convinced it was our lilo but, as I calculated its distance from the shore, I realised the futility of my trying to swim out to it.

Just behind me on the beach sat a young man – slim, dark-haired and with the sort of deep tan that only comes after months of Mediterranean sunshine. He was leaning possessively against a small red yacht and was equally possessively grasping a very beautiful young woman around her waist.

'Oh, monsieur,' I cried to him, 'mes enfants sont dans la mer sur un lilo. S'il vous plait pouvez-vous les sauver en votre bateau?'

He shook his head. 'Español,' he informed me sternly.

I began again, 'Senor, mis hijos están en el mar en un lilo—' My Spanish is even worse than my French. 'Por favor, usted in su barco—' What I hoped I was saying was, 'My children are in the sea on a lilo. Please can you save them in your boat?'

Some of my meaning must have got through to him, because reluctantly he got to his feet and began to push the yacht to the edge of the water. I prepared to join him but he shook his head. 'Con ella,' he said firmly, pointing to his nubile young companion.

'Con migo,' I implored.

'Con ella,' he repeated.

'Con migo,' I insisted – after all, they were my children, and while he might well prefer to be accompanied by a gorgeous young girl than by a mother of five, I felt that to be left to watch from the shore would be unbearable. For a moment he wavered, then 'Do you sail a boat?' he asked me in Spanish. This was the decider. I hadn't been on a yacht for fifteen years and then only as a passenger on board a very sizeable craft. It was my turn to shake my head. 'Con ella,' he repeated firmly and this time I didn't argue. The two of them set about launching the yacht and putting up its sails.

Meanwhile, as I stood anxiously watching the preparation, a portly French gentleman appeared beside me. 'Je nagerai vers vos enfants,' he said, and before I had time to utter more than, 'Mcrci, monsieur', he was gone – plunging into the sea and swimming strongly and steadily towards the distant lilo.

I stood watching him until his head was merely a speck in the water, and watched the yacht now fully launched with sails up moving off at a healthy pace. Jane came up to me. 'Come for a swim now, Mum?' she asked.

I rounded on her. 'Swim? Don't talk to me of swimming. Just you pray that your brother and your sisters aren't dead.'

'Oh, they aren't dead, Mum,' she replied thoughtfully. 'They're sitting back there with Dad.'

I stared in disbelief to where she was pointing. Then, realising that I had quite unnecessarily launched not only a yacht but also a middle-aged Frenchman, I slunk up the beach. 'Where were they?' I asked Wally.

'About a hundred yards down to the right of us,' he replied, 'at the edge of the water.' 'I called out to you,' he continued. 'What were you talking to that man about?'

'Under the circumstances,' I said, 'I think we had better stay well away from this section of the beach for the rest of our holiday.' I felt a complete idiot and could not face either the kindly Frenchman or young Spaniard again as neither in French nor Spanish would I have been able to offer any comprehensible explanation. We packed up quietly and stole away to our villa. However, I have often wondered what the young couple – as they undoubtedly were – harmlessly relaxing on their lilo, must have said when a portly French gentleman requested them to return at once to their mother, and a bright red yacht sailed up prepared to tow them in.

Following this incident, we took to selecting a spot at least two hundred yards further away from where the red yacht was normally pulled on to the beach. This was nearer to the pedalo hire point and resulted in frequent requests to take rides on them. They were strongly built and safe enough, but also rather expensive to hire so rides were not taken very often. However, one afternoon, Jane, Katie and I hired one so, with Jane and I pedalling, and Katie sitting in the middle, we headed off. It was amazingly easy to pedal and we sailed smoothly along the bay. I felt it would not be wise to go too far out from the shore so I intended pedalling along to the end of the beach, turning round and pedalling back again. We had been out for about ten minutes when Jane said, 'Look, we're at that big rock we see on the postcards.' I turned towards the beach.

We must have been travelling at a very good pace to have reached the end of the beach so quickly. We all studied the enormous rock – it stood about twenty-five feet high and was just one isolated rock in the whole of the otherwise sandy beach. It was quite a landmark and a good mile or so from where we normally sat, so we had never walked along to inspect it more closely. I then realised that we were all looking backwards at the rock and, despite the fact that Jane and I had stopped pedalling, we were still travelling at a fair speed and fast approaching the end of the beach. 'Pedal in reverse, Jane,' I ordered, and we both pedalled our hardest in reverse. The craft sailed steadily forwards, but at a marginally slower rate.

'Faster!' I shouted.

'I'm going as hard as I can,' Jane yelled back to me.

I considered the situation – obviously, unless we took some fresh course of action we would eventually drift around the end of the beach. High cliffs marked the end of it and these continued for a couple of miles until they softened a little to form a small cove. Unless we could turn the pedalo around and pedal it back before we had rounded the cliffs at the end of the beach, we had no way of reaching a shore for some time – and that was assuming that we could induce the thing to turn towards the shore. In this best-case scenario, we would be faced with a walk of several miles back to our own stretch of beach, shoe-less and wearing only our swimsuits – and I did not dare contemplate explaining to the pedalo owner the whereabouts of his property and how and why it was there. This was not an inviting prospect, and I tried to think of a more acceptable alternative.

I looked thoughtfully at Katie. 'Do you think you could swim to the beach and find Dad?' I asked her.

She hesitated for a moment. 'Why can't Jane go?' she asked.

'Because your legs won't reach the pedals of this thing,' I replied, 'and I can't pedal it on my own.'

Looking very doubtful, she slid off the pedalo and started swimming towards the shore. Jane and I pedalled furiously backwards all the time and watched her until we saw her reach the beach and wave to us before darting off in search of her father. We prepared for a long wait. Our one hour's hire had well and truly overrun. Nevertheless, although we were prepared to wait for Wally's arrival, it must have been another hour before we saw him striding along the beach with Katie running at his side. By this time, Jane and I felt as if our legs were almost falling off. We had pedalled continuously and constantly against the tide, but we derived a certain satisfaction from noting that our efforts had been worthwhile and we had only drifted a further hundred yards or so since Katie had left us. Wally plunged into the sea and swam towards us. He clambered on board. Wearily I explained the situation to him. He leaned over the back of the pedalo and grabbed a small handle.

'Why don't you use the tiller?' he asked me.

'What tiller?' I replied.

'This tiller,' he said, pulling the metal handle and simultaneously turning the pedalo around to face the opposite direction. I didn't bother replying – I was too exhausted anyway. Wally took over Jane's place and she sat on the middle seat, very glad of the rest. I pedalled on and, with a fresh set of legs, we quite quickly reached the pedalo landing spot. The owner had packed up for the day, so we pulled it up onto the beach ourselves.

'What took you so long?' I asked Wally.

'Katie didn't have her glasses on and so she couldn't see where we were sitting.'

Poor Katie. I could sympathise. She had had to go up to every group of people on the beach and peer at them from a yard or so away to check whether it was our family group. No wonder it took her so long. It took quite a long time for us to recover our land legs, and neither of us felt up to another pedalo trip for the remainder of our holiday.

Chapter 10

1971 – Return from Playo de Aro

We left Playa de Aro early in the morning in order to reach St Cere in good time for dinner. The journey went smoothly until mid-afternoon when the minibus developed an interesting knocking noise. We bore this for twenty miles or so, but then Wally decided that it was no longer to be ignored. Wally possesses a totally unjustified confidence in my A-level French. 'We'll stop at the next town,' he called to me, 'and you can explain what's wrong with the bus'. Now, my communications with the doctor in Sees the previous year had demonstrated that an appreciation of the French poets of the Romantic period and similar literary works is of little practical use in explaining medical matters, and I had no doubt that it would be of even less use in trying to explain anything technical relating to a car mechanic in a small town in southern France. However, upon consultation with Angela and Julia, both of whom had recently completed their O-level French exams, we came up with 'Il y a un defaut avec cette voiture': there is a fault with this car. Wally looked pained. 'If there wasn't a fault with the vehicle, we wouldn't be consulting him,' he pointed out – not altogether unreasonably. 'Can't you could say something a bit more technical?'

'What do you think is wrong with it?' I asked him.

'Just tell him there is a knocking under the offside front wheel,' he replied.

There was a stupefied silence from the rear of the bus as Angela, Julia and I sought desperately for the words. We searched our French phrasebook for a few helpful hints and were still constructing our sentence when we arrived on the outskirts of Villeneuve. It is a small town and it did not take us long to find its sole garage. Wally stepped down from the bus and, with a gesture to the young smiling mechanic, indicated that he had now divested himself of all responsibility for the vehicle and that we would explain the problem. I began my prepared speech. 'Notre voiture frappe au dessus la roue devant': 'our vehicle knocks under the front wheel'. The young man's smile faded and a faint expression of puzzlement crossed his brow which shortly turned to a look of total bewilderment. He shook his head, he shrugged his shoulders.

'I don't think he understands me,' I said.

Angela took up the cause. 'Un bruit semblable un frappe' (a noise like a knock), she began. It was quite evident that the young man had abandoned all pretence of following the train of explanation. He shook his head again and waved his arm from side to side, indicating that he could not understand a word . He turned to Wally who had, up to this point, not attempted one syllable in the way of describing the problem. He smiled at him and with his arms outstretched and fingers clenched around an imaginary wheel he steered an imaginary course. 'Oui?' he queried, moving towards the driving seat.

'I think he wants to drive,' I explained somewhat unnecessarily.

Wally looked a little hesitant.

'Oh, come on, it's the easiest way – Angela and I are never going to make him understand.'

Reluctantly, Wally joined the rest of us in the rear of the bus while our young French friend climbed into the driver's seat. As the rest of the family were settled in their seats, Wally decided to stand – not an easy feat for a tall man, but it had the dubious advantage of allowing him to watch the movements of the driver. We drove quite smoothly out of the small town and into the open countryside. After a mile or so, the now familiar knocking sound began again. Our driver's face lit up; he inclined his head towards the sound and he turned to us with his face wreathed in smiles. We smiled back. 'He's got it,' I said – a trifle superfluously. Our driver braked and the bus slowed down. We were travelling along a narrow straight road flanked by steep ditches. Our new friend began a three- (or, possibly, a seven- or seventeen-) point turn in order to drive back to the garage. It became clear that the minibus was almost exactly as long as the road was wide, not leaving a lot of room for manoeuvre. Nevertheless, it should have been possible, with care and moving very slowly, to turn round. Unfortunately, our driver was experiencing some difficulty in finding reverse gear. To begin with, he had thrust with confidence into what he had assumed was reverse and, as he came sharply off the clutch, the bus leaped forward several feet onto the grass verge. He shrugged his shoulders by way of apology and tried again – this time exercising a little more caution on the clutch. The bus moved inexorably forward again and the ditch loomed perilously near.

Now what Wally lacked in ability to communicate in French, he made up for by speaking Spanish. 'A la derecha,' he called to our driver. 'Reverser a la derecha.' The next movement of the bus made it clear to us all that the young man had totally failed to grasp that reverse gear was on the right. 'He must be a fool,' muttered Wally to all of us and then, in a loud and commanding tone, he called out again, 'A la derecha. Derecha. Reverser a la derecha.' It crossed my mind that addressing a garage mechanic from Villeneuve in Spanish was very much like addressing a garage mechanic from Birmingham in French. Meanwhile, the bus continued on its path. The driver made another attempt to find reverse gear and we all felt the front offside wheel exploring the edge of the ditch. Angela and I with one accord screamed 'Renverser à la droite!'

The young man turned to us. 'À la droite?' he queried.

'Oui, oui,' we answered, and with only the merest hint of resistance the wheel moved backwards away from the ditch.

A few more turns of the wheel and we were on our way back towards Villeneuve. The young man drove us into the garage and onto the ramp. He gestured that he would start work at once. It was very hot outside and the cool of the garage was most welcome.

'We might as well stay in the garage,' I said, 'everywhere is closed for siesta and it's too hot to walk very far. We'll have some food while we wait.' As I began to unpack some rolls and jam from our food basket, the bus began to rise steadily upwards and the younger children screamed with delight. That definitely settled where we would have our picnic, as none of the older members of the group felt like making an undignified leap to the ground, and the novelty of eating tea up on a ramp delighted the younger ones. The fault was put right in a very short time and we were on our way again. 'Can't understand why that fellow couldn't understand Spanish,' said Wally. 'We can't be more than two hundred miles from the Spanish border.'

We made an overnight stop in St Cere and next morning drove north to La Chartre-sur-le Loir, where we stopped for a second night. The following morning we all set off to visit the shrine of St Teresa at Lisieux, which was on our route to Le Havre. We spent a couple of hours there before heading towards Tancerville where an excellent restaurant had been recommended to us. It was our intention to have one really good meal together before catching the night boat from Le Havre. It was late afternoon when we called at the restaurant and booked a table for 7 p.m., which we felt would give us plenty of time to enjoy our meal and drive the twenty miles to Le Havre for the 10 p.m. boat. To fill in the two hours before our table booking, we drove to the local swimming pool, where the children enjoyed a good hour's swimming, and came back to the restaurant by 6.30 p.m. The children played on the swings and slide in the restaurant's garden until, on the stroke of 7 p.m., we made our way into the dining room and took our places at a long table at the end of the room. Time passed: ten minutes, twenty minutes…

Wally was beginning to get impatient but finally a waiter appeared and with many Gallic gestures explained that the delay was due to a large wedding party in the adjoining room – the guests had all arrived much later than expected and caused major staffing difficulties. Menus were placed before us, and still with a good hour and a half ahead to enjoy our meal, we all made our choices. Our order was taken and the waiter vanished again. By this time several other tables had been taken and we amused ourselves watching the reactions of the other diners as they passed from a stage of happy anticipation, through mild irritation and finally to outright impatience as they waited in vain for a sighting of a waiter.

At last another waiter appeared bearing two large baskets of rolls which he placed ceremoniously at either end of our table. We smiled smugly at our fellow diners. We waited for a further twenty minutes, the smugness fast fading. Wally was all for leaving without further ado, but was persuaded to stay a little longer. Then at 8.30 p.m. – an hour and a half after we had first sat down – our soup appeared. It was beautifully prepared and absolutely delicious, but hardly worth a ninety-minute wait. As we were all ravenous by now, we consumed it very quickly and sat waiting eagerly for our main course. Time passed, and at 9 p.m. our main meal arrived. Wally and the older children ate theirs at record speed while I spent the first five minutes cutting up meat for three-year-old Brendan. Having finished his meal, Wally stood up. 'We are leaving now,' he announced. 'We have a twenty-mile drive ahead of us and we have to pick up petrol. I'm not taking a chance on petrol stations being open early on Sunday morning at home.'

He signalled to a waiter and asked for the bill. Then, taking the two boys with him, off he went, leaving me to settle the bill and follow with the girls. The waiter was affronted to see us leaving so hastily and was especially offended by my untouched plate. He offered me alternative dishes, apparently incapable of grasping that it was the delay in serving the meal rather than the quality of the food which accounted for our hasty departure. Finally, he accepted that we were leaving and took the money offered. He stood aside in frosty silence as the girls filed out from behind the table. By this time the dining room was full and, following our recent verbal exchanges with the waiter over our leaving with food untouched, all attention was focused on us. As Julia sidled her way along the table, her jacket caught the large and beautifully crafted mustard pot and sent it crashing to the mosaic tiled floor. For a moment we all stood in horrified silence at the yellow spread and particles of china lying at our feet. Then, throwing caution and dignity to the winds, we ran from the room and rushed straight to the minibus. We collapsed in laughter.

'Do you think the waiter thought I did it deliberately?' she asked.

'I don't know,' I replied, 'but if the other diners see it as a way to protest over the service, that restaurant is going to have to replace a lot of mustard pots.'

Now all settled into the minibus we drove off towards Le Havre. We stopped at the first filling station and the attendant filled our tank. Wally paid and turned on the ignition switch. Nothing happened. He tried again – again nothing happened. No spark of life. Again and again he tried. The jovial mood of a few minutes earlier was gone. At last Angela gave voice to the thought that was in everyone's minds.

'What do we do now?' she asked.

I took command. 'We all sit very quietly and say three Hail Marys.'

'Now try it,' I said to Wally. He turned the key and the engine sprang into life immediately. Now, whether the three Hail Marys did the trick or whether the length of time it took the children to say them was just sufficiently long enough to drain a flooded carburettor, I do not know and will not try to guess. We were on the road again and bowling merrily towards Le Havre and our boat. The last few miles proved very tedious as the traffic was heavy, and the final fifteen minutes of our journey were extremely tense. We finally rolled through the car ferry gates at 9.59 p.m. and, as our back wheels touched the deck, the gates clanged shut. 'That,' said Wally, 'was too close for comfort and we are never stopping for a meal outside Le Havre again. From now on, it's sandwiches all round.' I could not help but agree.

Chapter 11

1973 – To Llafranch and back

In 1972, we stayed at home for the arrival of our daughter Helen, born in July. However, we decided that we would book another holiday in Spain for the following year, 1973. This time, there would be twelve in our party as Angela had become engaged to her boyfriend Richie and Jane had invited her close friend Hilary to join us. Our minibus, apart from its use on holidays and family excursions, had also been in daily use as a workhorse in our business and reluctantly we concluded that it was no longer reliable enough for a family trip to Spain. We had had quite enough difficulties in our travels without risking a total breakdown in a remote part of France. In anticipation we had bought a Peugeot estate car with sufficient seating room for eight or even nine (if they were small). (This was in the early 1970s, when seatbelts were not compulsory.) The sensible solution seemed to be for Wally and I and our six children to travel by car and for Angela, Richie, Teresa and Hilary to make their way by train. Train fares were considerably cheaper than

air fares in the 1970s. We timed our departures so that we would
arrive at our resort the night before and Wally would meet them
off the train early the next morning.

We were a little disappointed to learn that the villa we had so
enjoyed in Playa de Aro had been sold and the new owners were
not interested in renting it out, but our helpful agent offered us a
large apartment with five bedrooms in Llafranch which we felt
would suit us very well.

The journey to Llafranch remains – for me, at least – the
most trying of all we had made to date. We started well and
enjoyed a smooth and trouble-free run to Southampton.
However, as we waited to board the overnight ferry, Helen,
normally the most placid of babies, began to cry. I, by this time
a mother of six, needed no help in diagnosing the problem.
'She's cutting a back tooth,' I reported. Helen cried on. We
eventually boarded the ferry and found our cabins. Helen
continued to cry. There seemed little prospect of sleep for me,
so I sat on the edge of my bunk and nursed her. I found that
holding her in one particular position induced a fitful sleep, but
the least movement on my part resulted in a fresh outburst of
crying. And so the night passed. I was not in particularly good
shape to act as navigator the following morning, and Helen
made certain that I did not even try. Her tooth came through
early in the day as we drove through France, followed
immediately by a familiar red lump on the other side – a clear
sign that a second tooth was on its way through. Thus the crying
did not instantly cease, as I had so confidently predicted; if
anything, it reached an even greater crescendo. There were
moments of blessed peace, when, utterly exhausted, she dropped
off to sleep, but the slightest variation in sound – a change of
gear, a sudden braking, even conversation among the other
children – woke her up and the screaming would begin again.

We were very glad to reach St Cere and to be given a warm
welcome by the Bizats and we all hoped for a peaceful night – a
hope not to be realised for, as soon as the second tooth came

through, Helen set about cutting a third one and I found myself sitting up again all night – albeit in rather more comfortable surroundings. The next day's travel was even more tense and difficult than the previous one as the temperature was higher and tempers shorter. Helen's third tooth came through eventually, only to be followed immediately by a red lump signalling that her fourth one was on its way. At last, as we crossed the French–Spanish border, Helen broke into a wide smile, revealing four small white points in the corners of her mouth. Peace, blessed peace, was restored and Helen was her normal sunny self again. Even more amazingly, for once, our timing was perfect and we arrived in the early evening. The train bearing the other members of the group was also on time and, by mid-morning, we were all together and ready to explore our surroundings. Llafranch was a much smaller resort than Playa de Aro, which suited the younger children very well as they could wander around the little town on their own. The sandy beach was exactly thirty yards from our flat and, as it sloped very gently to the sea, ideal for the children.

It was a wonderful holiday, marred only by the non-appearance of our maid. Once again, being a large apartment, maid service for four hours a day had been added into the rent – this to include cooking a midday meal. Our maid appeared briefly on our first morning – a Saturday – and told us that she would be unable to undertake any cooking at all for the first week as she had to cover the duties of another maid who was ill. This seemed perfectly reasonable, if a little disappointing, but we decided to use the tins of meat we had brought with us and buy some local salad for that week to avoid having to stay indoors and cook. It seemed to me that the sick friend's workload must have been extensive for, as the week wore on, our maid's visits grew shorter and shorter. At last, on the following Saturday I managed to catch her on one of her flying visits. 'Next week cooking?' I asked, hopefully. She nodded vigorously. In my rudimentary Spanish I told her that on

Monday we would have a potato omelette with some green beans and I would buy everything. 'Lunes tortilla patata judías verdes y ha comprado todos.' As yet another salad appeared as our main meal, I was able to quell the more rebellious in the group by assuring them that on Monday cooked food was on the menu.

On Monday morning I bought three dozen eggs, a quantity of potatoes and some delicious-looking green beans and laid them on the kitchen table with a note stating that we would return at 1.30 p.m. for our lunch. 'Volver a la 1.30 p.m. para el almuerzo'. We all went off happily to the beach. At 1.15 p.m. we left the beach and, looking forward to our cooked meal, piled into the flat. What a terrible disappointment. Our eggs, beans and potatoes sat forlornly on the kitchen table, our rooms had not been touched and, worst of all, we had eaten the last of the tinned meat we had brought with us. As it was now siesta time, there was little likelihood of buying anything else. The light-hearted mood of moments earlier was gone. 'All hands on deck,' I called out and, while everyone went off to tackle their bedrooms and the living room, I, with a great deal of reluctance and deepest misgivings, set about converting the eggs and potatoes into a more edible state. As we ate our lunch, a few were heard to remark that they would never grumble about salads again.

It was now obvious that the maid was not going to provide the level of service to which we had become accustomed on our previous holidays (and, indeed, for which we had paid). This in itself was no hardship as far as the minimal housework was concerned, since in our party were a number of teenagers and some young adults – all perfectly capable of bed-making, dishwashing and floor sweeping. The cooking, however, was a minor irritation to me and to the rest of the group, who had to endure my efforts. I do not enjoy cooking at the best of times, and in a very small kitchen with the sun blazing down outside and a beautiful beach just thirty yards away, I gave it scant attention.

The almost total absence of the maid did throw up one other problem. We had brought three towels each – two for the beach and one for the flat. Thirty-six in total. In the halcyon days of Playa de Aro, the hard-working and much appreciated maid had always washed these for us and, believing that this would be the case here, we had used them recklessly so that by the end of our first week we had thirty-six dirty, sandy towels. Action had to be taken. I examined the sink – it was too small to even wash a hand towel. The apartment had two showers but no bath. A further search of the apartment uncovered a tin bath which seemed to be the obvious choice, but the prospect of hand-washing thirty-six bath towels was not appealing. Angela considered the problem with me. 'When I was in Naz,' she began, 'we used to tread on towels and sheets in the bath to wash them.' Angela had spent part of her early years in Nazareth House – a local Catholic children's home. I stared at her in disbelief. 'You've got to be joking,' I said. 'That's too Dickensian to be true.'

Angela laughed. 'No – we did it, honestly, before we had a washing machine. It was quite fun.'

It sounded anything but fun to me, but I was prepared to give it a try.

'Right,' I said. 'Let's get this bath onto the balcony, put on our bikinis and tread.' Teresa, also from Nazareth House, joined us and Angela was right: if not exactly fun, it was not really hard and we spent a highly productive morning treading towels in cold soapy water and deepening our suntans. I was also introduced to the Nazareth House method of wringing the towels. We took one end each and twisted in reverse directions, and very soon thirty-six towels were laid across the tables and chairs on our balcony. All were dry within two hours.

At lunch I spoke firmly to the family. 'From now on, only the very oldest towels are going to the beach and the proper

bathroom ones are never – repeat, *never* – leaving this flat.'
Going swimming several times a day, it was not going to be
easy to stick to this rule, but I was adamant, although it still
meant that Angela, Teresa and I spent a couple more mornings
treading towels before the holiday was over. Only on the last
but one day did I discover a launderette down a small side street
less than two hundred yards away! I thought it wise not to
mention this to anyone – especially not Angela and Teresa.

Towards the end of our second week the young German
family who had been occupying the flat above ours left for
home and Teresa told me that the new family were English. 'I'll
go up and call on them and see if there's anything they want,' I
said. I sauntered off and climbed the small flight of stone steps
leading to their flat. I knocked on the door. 'Hello,' I called. A
radio was playing. 'Hello,' I called again, stepping into the
hallway. In the kitchen I could see a blonde woman, her back
towards me, putting food away in the cupboard.

'I'm in the flat below and I—'

'Pat!' shrieked the woman, turning round.

'Gina!' I shrieked back.

By one of those strange quirks of fate, the flat above was
now being occupied by the very same friends whom we had met
in Playa de Aro three years before and had not seen since. My
family was totally mystified, when fifteen minutes later, I had
not returned. John came to find me and, to everyone's
frustration and bemusement, he also failed to return as he
renewed his friendship with their son. Finally, Wally decided to
solve the mystery and was equally delighted to see our new
neighbours – sensibly suggesting that we all go down to our sun
balcony and catch up on our news with a bottle of wine. As their
three children were of similar ages to our younger children, they
all made friends quickly and Llafranch will always hold very
happy memories for me.

During our stay there we learned that the Festival of the
Fishing Boats would be taking place in Palamós just seven

miles south and it was agreed that this was an event we should all experience. On the day of the festival all twelve of us piled into the car and drove to Palamós. Wally was not too enthusiastic about this family outing and left us on the quay, insisting that he had to go into Playa de Aro to telephone the office.

This is not as far-fetched as it must seem today. Playa de Aro boasted a new post office from which it was possible to place international calls with comparative ease. The post office in Llafranch opened only intermittently as the lady who ran it also had the ice-cream selling franchise for the surrounding villages. On warm days, which in mid-summer was every day, she pedalled off on her bicycle with a small portable fridge strapped on the front to sell her ices in these villages, returning to Llafranch and her post office only to restock her fridge. If it was inconvenient for anyone in Llafranch who needed to make an international call or even purchase a ten-peseta stamp, nobody felt the need to complain.

Once he had dropped us on the quayside in Palamós, Wally left for Playa de Aro. We were delighted at the sight before us. All the fishing boats in Palamós – at least fifty – were decorated from bow to stern in hundreds of small colourful flags. We watched with interest as a procession started along the quay – huge plaster models of a king and queen at least twelve feet high were carried along by young men, most of whom were wearing fancy dress. Whole families in fancy dress were already on board their boats. Then, to our amazement, we spectators were invited to climb aboard the boats for a trip out to sea and along the bay. We didn't hesitate and, selecting a large and comfortable-looking vessel, we all leaped on board – I clutching Helen. The boats left the shore, hooters blaring, and sailed out into Palamós Bay.

Once we were at sea the owner of our boat began passing around cans of beer which he had stowed on board. Presumably, in earlier times local wine would have been drunk but by 1973 beer had taken over as the favourite tipple. Music blared at top volume and, as the morning wore on, the young men in the boats began to compete to see who could dive the best. Eventually they were climbing to the tops of the masts and diving off, clean over the heads of the passengers on the decks. We sailed quite a distance and when we finally returned to shore, around three hours later, we found a thoroughly mystified and extremely concerned Wally pacing up and down the quay. Having left us on a crowded quayside with every berth occupied by a fishing boat, he returned to the entire place deserted and not a soul in sight. As he told us later, thoughts of the *Marie Celeste* or 'close encounters' crossed his mind.

When we began planning this particular holiday, we thought we would add some educational interest and we decided to spend a couple of days visiting some of the better-known châteaux in the region. On the two previous occasions we had driven straight through the château region and never so much as sighted one. I had researched hotels in the area via my trusty French motoring handbook (since there was no internet access in 1973) and selected a hotel in Amboise, Hotel du Gare. I wrote to the hotel and reserved two family rooms. In due course the reply came, confirming our booking. Curiously, it was addressed to 'Monsieur and Madame Yours Faithfully'. I assumed that, having typed the letter, I had forgotten to sign my name. Wally conjectured that, given my handwriting, they had probably assumed it was some Celtic symbol of goodwill.

We began our châteaux tour at Chenonceaux – surely the most beautiful of all – which is set on a lake which, on this sunny day, reflected it in its entirety. Being used to the fully furnished stately homes of Britain, we were a little disappointed to find the rooms virtually bare but concluded that, following the French Revolution, all such homes would have been ransacked. From Chenonceaux we made our way to Amboise, arriving in plenty of time to visit the château there in the centre of the town before finding our hotel. Given its name, this presented no difficulty and it appeared that the rear portion of the hotel building was in fact the booking office and waiting room for the railway station.

As it had been several months since I had made our reservation, I had completely forgotten about the oddly addressed reply. We made our way through the front door. There really could have been no doubt that we were the party from Britain who had reserved two family rooms. The lady owner greeted us with a wide smile. Gesturing that she did not speak English, she pushed the hotel register towards me for me to sign us all in. And there it was, written clearly and boldly: the 'Yours Faithfully' family booked into rooms 5 and 6. I felt that any alteration or even an attempted explanation in my barely comprehensible French would probably be useless and may well lose us our reservation so, taking up the proffered pen, I signed the register. W. Yours Faithfully, P. Yours Faithfully and carried on with J. S. K. J. B. and H. Yours Faithfully. The lady seemed satisfied with this and led us to adjoining rooms, both with beautiful pine polished floors, comfortable-looking beds and a wash-basin and bidet in the corner. With Jane, Sarah and Katie in one, Wally, the three youngest children and I began to settle ourselves into the other.

The older girls were told to wash and change into clean clothes for dinner and, while Wally took John and Brendan to have a drink at the small tables in the garden outside, I concentrated on changing Helen and attempting a modest improvement to my own appearance, until I heard shrieks coming from the adjoining room. Hastily rushing in, I discovered that we had done it again. This time it was Jane who was responsible. Confronted by a bidet for the first time in her life, she had presumed it was a foot bath and decided to wash her feet in it. She had turned the taps on fully but found she was unable to turn them off again. The plughole was far too small to cope with the volume of water from the two fully open taps, and the result was a steady flow of water spreading over the brilliantly polished floor. My first efforts at wrestling with the taps failed hopelessly, but eventually with a burst of brute force I managed it. Meanwhile Helen had decided to crawl in to investigate so that, in addition to a very wet floor, I now also had a very wet baby.

It was time to get reinforcements. Sarah was sent to haul Wally away from his drink. Having viewed the scene for a few minutes, he hit upon a solution for mopping the floor. In a suitcase on top of the car was a large case packed full of the thirty-six towels on their way to my washing machine at home. They were immediately brought into active service and did an excellent job of drying the floor. After the mopping up was complete, we wrung them out in a rather half-hearted manner before hurling them back into the case.

Washed and brushed, we all went down to the garden for a drink before dinner. Wally sat there thoughtfully. 'Hotel du Gare,' he pondered. 'Means Station Hotel, doesn't it?'

I agreed.

'That probably explains why an express train tears through every four and a half minutes – on average.' To confirm this, a huge train thundered past us, shaking the glasses on the table and causing an empty Coca-Cola bottle to fall off and smash on the floor.

'I wouldn't mind betting they run all through the night,' he continued gloomily. He was absolutely right – but we calculated that around 3 a.m. the time between each train decreased to every seven minutes.

Drinks finished, we made our way towards the dining room where the main meal was fish. Wally was extremely fond of fish and I have no particular objection to it, but Jane, Sarah, Katie and John loathed it, so toyed with their meal. Brendan found that he simply loved it, and ate not only his own meal but also those of his siblings. We all sat there, trying to be inconspicuous in the small but crowded dining room, when suddenly a drop of water landed on the floor next to where John was sitting. We looked up and saw another drop forming and preparing to fall. A quick calculation of the position of the girls' bedroom on the first floor in relation to our position in the dining room on the ground floor made the cause obvious. Jane's little experiment with the bidet, flooding the bedroom, was about to make itself all too evident. I hissed at John, 'Drop your napkin on the floor where the water is falling.' Obediently he did so and for the rest of the meal we were at least free of the embarrassing sound of splashes. We made our way from the dining room as soon as was decently possible. Perhaps future hotel reservations by our family should carry a flood warning!

The children slept well but Wally and I resolved that before we booked into a hotel again we would take into account the English translation of its name and any possible implications. The following morning we set off again, visiting the chateau at Blois – especially interesting for its superb external staircase – before heading north to Le Havre and home.

Chapter 12

1975 – To Spain by French Rail

After eighteen months at home (no holiday in 1974), the lure of hot sun and warm sea persuaded us to plan yet another trip to Spain, in 1975. For reasons that escape me, we decided to try both a different agent and a different means of travel through France. Subsequent events proved both decisions to have been seriously misguided.

First, with regard to our means of travel, Wally, with the memory of long hours spent at the wheel with sun blazing down on the narrow winding roads, suggested that we try French Rail. At that time French railways were running a highly successful advertising campaign urging unsuspecting Britons to put their cars onto French trains and travel in comfort on the train across France. Having travelled by train to both Italy and Spain in earlier year, I had some misgivings.

'Nonsense,' said Wally. 'You've got no idea what the trains are like today.'

I remarked acidly that the time to which I was referring was less than twenty years ago.

'French trains are magnificent,' enthused a colleague at work, 'and the food is out of this world'.

I wondered if he could have been referring to some pre-war era and a journey on the Orient Express, but realised that he was not old enough to have experienced that. Therefore the decision was taken – French Rail it would be.

By this time, Angela and Richie had married and Teresa was old enough to holiday with friends of her own age, so the number in our party was reduced to Wally, me, our six children and Louise, a friend of Sarah. We made our booking. We would drive to Folkestone and cross the Channel on the ferry to Boulogne. Here we would drive our car onto the train which would carry us across France overnight while we, after a delicious dinner on the train, would sleep soundly in our sleeping compartment. After a French breakfast eaten while travelling through a picturesque part of France we would arrive at Avignon refreshed and ready to commence the last leg of our journey – a six-hour drive into Spain. We made and paid for our bookings to include two adjacent sleeping compartments and dinner and breakfast for all nine of us to be taken on the train.

That was the plan. Reality proved very different. The first leg of the journey went smoothly. Admittedly, in that pre-M25 age, we had to leave home at 4 a.m. in order to be certain of arriving at Folkestone in time to catch the noon ferry, but there was at least the prospect of a pleasant afternoon on the boat and an evening on the train. The second part of the journey also passed without a hitch and we arrived at Boulogne at 4 p.m. There was a little confusion at this stage over where the loading point for our car was to be found, but this was eventually sorted out. As the loading of cars was not due to begin until 6 p.m. we assumed we could leave our car in line and take a walk around the town. However, this was not so at all. We were told that the driver had to remain in the car. Wally therefore stayed in the car while the rest of us humped our overnight cases from the car and set off to explore the station and immediate surroundings. The prospect of trailing seven children around Boulogne without Wally's support held little attraction for me, so we settled ourselves on our cases on the platform and tried to amuse ourselves watching the general bustle around us

After a little while our train drew in and we were able to find our reserved seats and sleeping accommodation. At this point I went along to the dining car to make a reservation for dinner, to be informed that breakfasts only were served on this particular train but, when I produced the nine vouchers for dinner, I was told that they could be used in the station restaurant. So, leaving the older children in our compartment, I took Brendan and Helen with me to find Wally and discuss the matter. When I reached him the cars were just beginning to board. 'We'll eat in the station restaurant,' he called out. 'We've got plenty of time – the train doesn't leave until 8 p.m.' We trekked back to our compartment. 'Come along,' I said encouragingly, 'we're going to have dinner here in the station.' Five faces fell.

'At the station?' they queried.

'How dull.'

'You promised we were going to have dinner on the train.'

'I'm not hungry.'

Signs of rebellion were afoot. 'For heaven's sake, come along!' I cried in exasperation. 'You're lucky I found out now before the train leaves. At least we'll all eat and it should be very nice.'

The Boulogne station restaurant was elegant enough. It had an Edwardian atmosphere and a very comprehensive menu, ideal for adults with an evening to spare, but rather too refined and too sophisticated for our young family. The rather sober atmosphere was not helped by the fact that we were the only ones in the restaurant. Having now loaded our car safely onto the train, Wally joined us and we began to make a selection from the menu. What was on offer was reasonably priced and there was a good variety. The fault lay entirely in our young family's failure to appreciate the cuisine. Eventually we decided that we would all begin with Parma ham and follow this with coq au vin for the children and a delicious-sounding veal dish for Wally and me. Speed of service was not a priority in the restaurant, and we had to wait a long time before our Parma ham was placed before us. It was delicious, and Wally and I soon finished ours. John and Brendan looked at theirs doubtfully at first but, once persuaded to try it, they enjoyed it, and the girls had no problem in finishing theirs in record time so, happy and relaxed, we eagerly anticipated our main course. It was not to be. The next moment there was an announcement. 'I think they're calling for passengers to Avignon,' said Wally. We called our waiter, who spoke excellent English, and he confirmed our suspicions. 'Oui, monsieur, all passengers for Avignon must board at once.' We explained that we were bound for Avignon and, with the greatest reluctance, parted with the nine pre-purchased vouchers and rushed from the restaurant to the platform where our train was standing. 'We haven't had our drinks,' complained John. True enough. They had been ordered to arrive with our main meal. 'Never mind, we'll get some drinks once we're on board,' I reassured him. We settled ourselves into our compartment and waited for the train to leave. We waited and we waited. During the time we waited we could have finished our main course, eaten dessert and had time for coffee and liqueurs. The buffet bar and restaurant were next to our carriage but the door was firmly locked. 'They'll open the bar once the train is moving,' Wally stated with confidence.

The train eventually started, but the bar remained steadfastly locked. Enquiries made with the ticket collector confirmed my worst suspicion – the restaurant and bar would not open before breakfast next morning. I appreciate that deprivation of drink is a suffering which has been experienced by many, such as those crossing a desert or perhaps in a siege. In such circumstances, I am sure it is possible to bear the suffering and feel heroic. It is not possible to feel the least so when crossing France by train on a family holiday. We felt indignant and angry. The train, so we discovered, was a through train to Avignon with no stops on the way. The children's clamours for drinks increased. Wally went off to find out at what time breakfast would be served. 'Breakfast starts at 6 a.m.,' he told me. 'So we had all better be up in good time to be sure of getting the first sitting.' Eventually we all settled down for the night. It was very hard to convince Brendan and Helen that the water from the wash-basin tap was not drinking water, as the sight of it only increased their thirst.

As the train sped through the night it gathered speed. I lay in my bunk as it swayed alarmingly from side to side and recalled, with grave misgivings, a true story told to me by a college friend. Some years earlier, he and his friend had been travelling to Italy via Paris. In Paris they had a few hours to wait for their train to Italy and they spent this time in the station bar in the company of a jovial Frenchman clad in the blue dungarees and black beret normally associated with a French worker. He introduced them to a cheap brandy which he was drinking in vast amounts. Finally, in an alcoholic haze, they realised that the arrival of their train was being announced. All three staggered to their feet. My friend and his companion bade goodbye to their drinking partner and made their way to their compartment. As they climbed aboard they spotted him clambering into the engine driver's cab! My friend spent a very uncomfortable night. His head throbbed remorselessly and when it did momentarily clear, the realisation that the engine driver had drunk even more than he had was so horrific that the throbbing itself provided welcome relief.

This story spun round and round in my head as we hurtled across France. I must have fallen into a fitful sleep as I was suddenly awoken by a tremendous crash nearby. Oh my God. It's happened! I thought – truly believing that the train had crashed.

Wally, John and Brendan sat up. Wally slid open the

compartment door and looked out. All along the corridor, passengers were crowding out of their compartments. There were comparatively few English people on board; there were many French, some Germans, some Belgians and two Dutch. We all looked at each other and in a variety of languages asked each other what had happened. There were expressions of surprise – even shock – and a few expressive shrugs of shoulders and shakings of heads. One man, a German, opened the window fully and stuck his head and shoulders out looking up and down the outside of the train (although, as the train was still speeding along, I could not imagine what he expected to see). Finally, the door to the compartment next to ours slid open. Sarah poked her head out. She was grinning from ear to ear. 'Did you hear it, Mum?' she asked. 'Katie fell off her bunk – it made an awful noise.'

I turned towards her 'Is Katie all right?' I asked.

'Fine,' replied Sarah. 'She didn't wake at first but I thought I'd better try and wake her in case she was unconscious, and now she's climbed back into her bunk.'

I felt that there could not be much wrong with any child who could so easily climb back into a bunk and, as I looked along the corridor, in which even more passengers had now gathered, I realised that my first priority was to calm their fears. I took a deep breath. 'Ma petite fille est tombé hors du lit.' Understanding dawned on a few faces – those who had managed to understand my accent. The German was not so easily won over and kept addressing me in German. 'My little girl fell out of her bunk,' I said loudly and clearly, 'and I am afraid that I do not speak German.' Drawing myself up to my full 5 feet 4 inches, I squared my shoulders and marched resolutely back into our compartment.

Sleep was slow in returning and it seemed that I had barely shut my eyes before Wally was standing over me and shaking me. 'It's five o'clock,' he said to me. 'Better get the children up and dressed so that we can be sure of being among the first for breakfast.' I forced myself out of my bunk, called the girls in the adjoining compartment, washed and dressed and set about getting John, Brendan and Helen ready.

With the prospect of food and, more importantly, drink before them, all the children were up and dressed in record time and by 5.40 a.m. we were all gathered outside the door to the restaurant car. It was still locked. 'Of course,' said Wally, 'they won't open it until 6 a.m.' Over the next fifteen minutes, we were joined in the corridor by fifty or sixty fellow passengers, all with the same objective in mind. Shortly before 6 a.m., a tantalising aroma of freshly brewed coffee wafted from under the door, together with the smell of newly-baked bread. I knocked on the door. There was no reply. Five minutes passed and I knocked again. By now it was 6.15 a.m. We heard the clatter of cutlery and the clink of china and could even make out the murmuring of voices from some happy and probably well-fed passengers beyond the locked door. Before I had a chance to knock again, a small but determined French woman came steaming past us and in a most peremptory manner hammered on the door shouting, 'Ouvrez la porte. Ouvrez la porte.' Much good did it do her. The door remained closed. However, she did not admit defeat easily. She hammered again and eventually a man's voice was heard from the other side. I make no claim to be able to understand even half of what is said to me in French, but I was able to recognise only too easily the words 'première classe'. Breakfast on the train was for first-class passengers only! It is extremely difficult to adequately express anger and frustration through a solid locked door – especially when one is not fluent in the language. One of our fellow passengers set off in search of some official help and returned followed by a small bustling official who, after closely examining the nine vouchers which we had purchased for breakfast on the train, told us that they could be used at the station restaurant at Avignon. 'What time do we arrive at Avignon?' we asked him. 'Nine o'clock,' he replied and retreated as quickly as he could.

We returned to our compartment. It was now 6.30 a.m. and we still had two and a half hours to get through. The children sat in sullen and sulky silence as we all stared out of the window at the passing scenery. Suddenly, to our horror, we saw a train overtaking us two tracks away. On its transporter was our car – not, I hasten to add, just our car but every other car which had been loaded on at Boulogne and which, up until that moment, we had felt happily confident were all trundling along behind us. The sight of their vehicles disappearing away from them galvanised all the other passengers to rush into the corridor. Windows were opened and heads thrust out – the German first.

There were agonised shouts in all languages: 'My car,' 'Ma voiture,' 'Mein auto.' Consternation all round. Finally, the bustling official appeared. He was obviously well used to this reaction. It surely must have happened on every journey. He explained patiently that our cars were now taking a slightly more direct route to Avignon – for goods trains only – and by the time we arrived our cars would have been offloaded and would be waiting for us in the station car park. Duly mollified, we all returned to our compartments. The next two hours dragged past. Seven very hungry children were in no mood to appreciate the magnificent scenery. At last, at nine o'clock we reached Avignon. The first part of the train official's prediction had come true – our cars had indeed arrived – but the second part had not lived up to expectation. All the cars were still parked on the transporter. The queue for breakfast was a long one. Our compartment was near the rear of the train, from which we struggled, hampered by the size of our party and our overnight baggage, and found ourselves at the end of the breakfast queue. But we did eventually reach the counter and were gratefully seated at two adjacent tables in the small garden outside the restaurant where we could savour our fresh orange juice, hot coffee and newly-baked croissants while watching the business of unloading the cars from the train.

As I sat watching this operation, my delight at finally sitting down to my long-awaited coffee and croissants vanished. It seemed that the average age of the boys who were employed to drive the cars off the transporters could not have been more than twelve. Surely it should be illegal to employ young persons in such a job? It was probably criminal – more for the damage they were doing to the cars than for any injuries they might sustain themselves. They had a unique method of unloading. They started the cars on the narrow rails on the transporter and drove along, these accelerating as much as possible so that they were achieving a speed of almost sixty miles an hour as they hurtled down the ramp. With a squealing of tyres, they turned sharply to the right and into the station car park. A screech of brakes signified a car parked successfully. The child at the wheel of our car looked about eleven, his head barely visible above the steering wheel. I closed my eyes, opening them only when I heard the squeal of brakes followed by a blessed silence. I then turned to watch the reaction of our German fellow traveller as his brand new Mercedes was driven off in a similar manner: apprehension, anger, terror and, finally, relief.

Now that breakfast was over and our car safely off the train there was nothing to keep us in Avignon, and so we piled our luggage into the boot and all climbed into the car with spirits high once again as we prepared for the last leg of our journey.

It all began so well, with the prospect of an easy run to Puerto de la Selva which lay only a short distance over the Spanish border. We started by taking the autoroute out of Avignon. We had not travelled on French motorways on our previous journeys to Spain and found it quite pleasant and relaxing, despite the high volume of traffic. The autoroute at this time did not continue into Spain so, as we approached its end, we had to decide which route we should take to our resort. After a few moments studying the map I said that as it was so near the French border and as we had driven along the inland road on our other journeys, it would be a pleasant change to take the coast road from Perpignan. From the map it looked a shorter route than taking the main road, being shown as approximately thirty-one miles. Regrettably, the map was unable to warn us of the road conditions.

Ignorant of what lay before us, we set off. The first fifteen miles were on a straight and comparatively quiet road and we were delighted to see the Mediterranean lying several hundred feet below us on our left. On the right a wall of rock towered above us. The road itself formed a narrow break between the sheer drop into the sea below and the endless expanse of rock. It was exactly wide enough for two cars to pass without actually forcing one to drop into the sea or the other to crush on the rock face.

Once the straight stretch ended, the road became an almost perfect corkscrew, never letting the driver see much more than twenty yards ahead as it twisted its way around the cliffs. Such roads were not unknown to us as we had driven along similar ones in the Dordogne region of France. Those roads were normally deserted and we were able to travel along them at a leisurely pace, even admiring the scenery. This road, on the contrary, was frighteningly busy. A constant stream of traffic kept hurtling towards us at every bend. At one point, to add to what was already a difficult situation, a large black Mercedes caught up with us and began to try to overtake. Wally, normally a patient driver and tolerant of others' faults and foibles, became increasingly irritated. 'The man is a fool,' he muttered. 'He is a raving lunatic.' The Mercedes edged its way around the tail of our car, only to pull back as a large truck, driven with the happy abandon of most Spanish truck drivers, raced towards us around the next bend.

'Oh God, he's trying to kill us!' I yelled and, turning to face the back window of our car, I flapped my hands up and down at the driver of the Mercedes. It is extremely doubtful if he understood the gesture. He certainly ignored it. Time and time again he tried to pass us. There was simply no room for us to pull over and allow him to do so, and he seemed oblivious to the unending stream of traffic coming towards us. At last we saw a tiny lay-by and pulled into it, allowing him to overtake us.

The children, meanwhile, remained blissfully oblivious to any potential danger, being fully absorbed in hand-held puzzles, comics and word games. After this, the journey continued smoothly, although It took us almost six hours to cover the comparatively short distance from the border to our resort – a journey which, we later learned, would have taken under two hours along the inland route. However, we got there at last and I went off to find the agent to collect the key to our apartment.

She was ready for us and jumped into her own small car to lead us there. Puerto de la Selva is not a very large resort, so within a few minutes she had stopped in a small square near the church. She pointed to a building on a hill about a hundred feet above us. 'That is it,' she said. Our eyes followed the direction in which she was pointing. Then we looked at the route that she was telling us to take. It was a stretch of cobbled steps – albeit very wide and shallow steps – but unmistakably steps. 'What do we do about the car?' we asked her. She shrugged her shoulders expressively. 'There is a car park,' she replied, waving her arm in the opposite direction to the flat. 'You can't park here,' she added, pointing to the 'Parking Prohibited' signs all around the tiny square.

Wally and I looked at each other. We considered the problem of carrying all our luggage, including numerous boxes of tinned food, from a car park of unknown location to the apartment at the top of the cobbled steps.

'Shall we try it?' asked Wally.

'I think she'll make it,' I replied and our loyal and dutiful Peugeot 504 family estate car, like a well-schooled steeplechaser, pawed at the ground once or twice and then skilfully and nimbly leaped up the steps, coming to rest on a patch of grass under a laburnum tree. I resisted the temptation to tether it to the tree, and began unloading. A hundred feet directly below us, our agent stood staring in disbelief. I waved to her. 'Thank you!' I called, and turned into the apartment.

Chapter 13

1975 – Puerto de la Selva and home

Puerto de la Selva was a disappointment to us. If poetic licence had been used in describing our bungalow in Port Isaac as being 'two minutes from a sandy beach', the author was an absolute beginner compared with the one who had written the description of our apartment in Puerto de la Selva. There was indeed a sandy beach, and it may well have been only a two-minute walk – if you were alone, late at night. It was at the bottom of a very steep hill flanked on both sides by small shops displaying most of their goods outside. Trailing a party of children and all their beach accessories made it a lengthy and tedious trip in both directions.

Once we had unpacked and had a meal, we set off to explore. The promised beach was tiny and every available inch either taken up by fishing boats or fishing nets which elderly men sat repairing. It was very picturesque, but by no means ideal for a family with seven children. However, we were told that there was a much larger sandy beach five minutes' walk away. As it was getting rather late, we decided to leave it until the following morning.

The next day, we set off for the promised beach. It was large, but the sand was mixed with mud and the beach had a very gentle slope so that the sea disappeared rapidly into the horizon. When we arrived, it was probably almost half a mile away, which did not lend itself to easy swimming. Determined to make the best of it, we settled on the beach but soon noticed a particularly unpleasant smell. This, we discovered, was because the main sewer for the town ran through the beach and into the sea! By now we were thoroughly disenchanted, but were advised that if we walked in the opposite direction from our apartment along the top of the ridge, we would find a lovely clean beach.

The next morning, we went in search of it. Twenty-five minutes later, we reached it, as it involved clambering over several large rocks set into the pathway. An able-bodied person unencumbered by all the children's beach paraphernalia would probably have managed it in half that time, but not us. It was a delightful little cove, and the sea was clear and the older children immediately put their snorkel masks and flippers to good use. Sadly for Brendan and Helen, there was not a grain of sand in sight. As they were unable to swim with any real competence, they had to content themselves with exploring the small rock pools. Later that afternoon we discovered yet another unwelcome feature of the resort. Practically every day at about 4 p.m., large rainclouds would gather over the nearby mountains and head in the direction of Puerto de la Selva.

Once they had reached their target, they would release a persistent deluge of rain for about thirty minutes. The clouds would then clear, leaving the evening filled with sunshine. The consequence of this was that we had to make sure we had packed up and left the rocky beach by 3.30 p.m. – and even then we were once caught out by the arrival of the deluge a little earlier, while we were still battling our way along the rocky ridge path.

One of the attractions that had drawn us to this resort was that the brochure promoting it promised that there were bicycles for hire. Apart from Helen, all the children could ride bikes, and the prospect of exploring some of the small lanes and coastal paths seemed most appealing. So, on our fourth day, armed with directions to the bicycle hire shop, we all set off. We were a little bemused to discover that the address we had been given was now a shop selling small electrical goods. We asked the owner where we could find the bicycle hire shop, but he looked at us scornfully and told us that the bike-hire business had closed four or five years earlier! Back we went to our rocky beach.

Another attraction of the resort mentioned in the brochure was horse-riding. Again all the children rode (with the exception of Helen), and Katie was especially looking forward to this aspect of the holiday. On our brief visit to the malodorous beach, I had noticed a sign pointing up a country lane which clearly stated – in English – 'Horse Riding'. The very next day we had an early lunch and set off in search of the horses. We walked up this narrow lane for about two miles until we finally saw ahead of us a gate, beyond which were some timber buildings, obviously stables. We quickened our pace and the most eager ran ahead. A disappointment lay in store for us. A notice hung on the gate stating – again in English – 'Horses have moved to Cebere' – a town about ten miles away, but as far as we were concerned they could have moved to Siberia – we certainly were not going riding this holiday.

During the second week of our stay, a funfair came to town. It was by anyone's standards a very modest one, consisting of a roundabout for very young children and a small dodgem track, plus two or three prize-vending machines into which unlimited coins could be fed without ever grabbing any item which you might conceivably want. However, at this stage of the holiday a rocking horse or a seesaw would have proved a welcome diversion.

On the day after our first visit to this fair, Katie came to me in great distress – she could not find her purse, which contained all her spending money to buy gifts and souvenirs – and she thought she had left it in the dodgem car. It contained 1000 pesetas (about £6). It was with little optimism that we went back to the fair that evening and I asked the woman running the dodgem cars if she had found a purse. With a broad smile, she went straight to her tiny office and brought out the small red purse, with all the money still inside. Our faith in human nature was restored ten-fold.

Despite this, it was with no great regret that we finally packed for home. There, we lived less than ten miles from a sandy beach (although, admittedly, to swim in the cold, murky sea did require a degree of courage, and there was no guarantee of sunshine). However, within three miles of our home there was an excellent riding centre with a large indoor arena, and furthermore in our own garden shed there were several bicycles – a few were missing some minor accessories, such as a pedal or a saddle – but they were quite good enough for our needs.

The disappointments of the holiday meant that we were actually looking forward o the journey home and to a visit we intended to make en route. During the winter months we had watched a programme on television about the 'lost treasure of Jerusalem', which had supposedly been buried in the area around Carcassonne. The programme had focused on a tiny hamlet called Rennes-le-Chateau, which was believed to be the final resting place of the treasure. Our train was due to leave from Narbonne for Calais and, as our route took us within a few miles of this hamlet, we decided to make a diversion and visit it.

If our journey to Puerto had at times been fraught with discomfort and frustration, these faded into insignificance beside the events that occurred on our journey home. It began well enough. We had already decided that we would take the inland route rather than risk the picturesque but highly hazardous coast road, and we drove happily along with Rennes-le-Chateau in our sights. Unfortunately, our map was too small a scale to show this tiny village, and we drove around the area for two hours repeatedly asking for directions.

We found Rennes-les-Bains easily enough and were directed from there to take what was virtually a bridle path across open fields and mountains. We did not dare try to follow this route, since to break down in such an isolated spot would have been disastrous. It seemed likely that days could pass before help would come by. Finally, we had to admit defeat and turned to retrace our tracks.

We could not risk missing our train out of Narbonne at 4 p.m. We had taken care to buy some bread, fruit and cheese in a small town on our way, and we were travelling along a country road about ten miles from Narbonne when we realised that there was a queue of cars in front of us. We slowed down and crawled along behind it. I said, 'It looks as if there has been an accident,' and got out of the car to investigate. I had only taken a few steps when a French woman rushed towards me shouting 'Le pont est poof!' and, to add clarity to this statement, she flung her arms up and outwards: 'Les Basques!' she shrieked, 'le pont est poof.'

'I think she's trying to tell us that the Basques have blown up the bridge,' I said to Wally. He expressed horror at the prospect of our missing our train. I grabbed the map –which had proved so ineffective at locating Rennes-le-Chateau – and discovered that if we took a left turn up a small country lane, and then a right turn, we would arrive in Narbonne, approaching from the west rather than the south.

Luckily, this turning was just a few hundred yards ahead and with great relief we turned into it. It was an extremely narrow lane and we travelled very cautiously. Within a few miles we came to a crossroads with a signpost clearly indicating that

Narbonne was to our left. This did not tally in the least with our map, and I was sure it was wrong. Then I saw an elderly man sitting on the grass verge a little way from the signpost. I asked him in my excruciating French which was the direction for Narbonne. 'Quelle direction est Narbonne?' and he pointed in the direction shown by the sign. Wally was convinced by this, but I was sure that I was right.

'He probably didn't understand me,' I said, 'or he doesn't know the area himself.'

I managed to persuade my husband to follow my directions and within twenty minutes I was gratified to see a sign before us announcing that we were at Narbonne. We later learned that it was not the Basques who had blown up the bridge, but a group of French wine-growers who were deeply dissatisfied with the low prices their wine was currently commanding. To add to the confusion they were causing by blowing up the bridge, they had also arranged for some of their supporters to turn the road signs around!

By now it was 3 p.m. and, as there seemed to be no sign of our train, we parked in the car park and headed towards our platform. Narbonne station had three platforms serving four lines of rail track. However, only the first platform nearest to the town had any toilet facilities, restaurant or food and drink kiosk. It was from this platform that our train was due to depart. It was extremely crowded when we made our way on to it, with the reason for this soon becoming obvious. A train had arrived from Paris with a party of fifty Italian school girls accompanied by two nuns. They had made straight to this first platform to take advantage of the facilities. We looked around and settled ourselves on the platform; and I mean literally on the platform as the three benches were fully occupied. As we sat there, we saw another train pulling in on another track. It had also come from Paris en route to Marseilles, and from it a party of twelve Algerians stepped down, all dressed in flowing robes and traditional headgear. We watched in fascination and disbelief as they started searching around the station area, collecting small pieces of wood. They piled these up at the end of the platform quite close to us and set them alight. Then, as the fire began to burn to their satisfaction, they opened a bag and took out some meat and long skewers to begin cooking themselves a meal. It had a most appetising smell – we felt our cheese and rolls came in a poor second.

Time passed. Four o'clock came and went, as did five o'clock and six o'clock. By now we had finished all our food and also the four litres of orange squash which we had prudently brought from Puerto. I set off in search of further food or drink but, by now, both the restaurant and the food kiosk had closed, having run out of supplies due to the unusual demands made on them by the ever-increasing numbers who had been forced to abandon their trains.

The two nuns tried to keep control of their charges, but I felt that they were losing the struggle. A German woman with five children in tow approached me and asked if I knew where the train to Dusseldorf was. She must have sensed a kindred spirit in me as, although I spoke no German and she no English, I remembered seeing a train marked 'Dusseldorf' pull in three tracks away and confidently led her to her train. At least she could settle the children in some comfort. We, meanwhile, had seen nothing of our train to Boulogne. The evening wore on. The Algerians, anxious not to let their fire go out, had now begun dismantling the small white picket fence which separated the platform from the pavement outside. I wondered, if they had to spend the night on the platform, whether, having exhausted their wood supply from the fence, they would begin dismantling the station building itself.

Finally, at 9 p.m., we were told that our train was now pulling in and we could load our car on to the transporter and find our seats. Of course, we had expected to be travelling through the day and had made sleeping reservations on the night ferry from Calais – which was due to arrive in Dover in the

early morning, seeing us back home in the mid-afternoon.
Having loaded the car, we found our compartment and settled
down. The children dropped off to sleep quite easily, even
sitting upright. Wally and I were not so fortunate, and the night
was very long.

The journey from Narbonne to Calais should have taken
about six hours. I don't know if blowing up the bridge had
caused major diversions throughout the region, but I do know
that at 7 a.m. we were still travelling somewhere in northern
France. The train stopped at a small station. We heard a
commanding voice call out, 'Café, café,' and, looking out of the
window, we saw an amazing sight. Striding along the platform
was a chef, clad in white catering coat and tall chef's hat,
followed by a small boy wearing a white apron that reached his
ankles and a white cotton beret at a rakish angle. He was
carrying a yellow plastic bucket in which lay the vaunted 'café'.
Only the French would have the chutzpah to announce coffee
served in a yellow plastic bucket as if they were bringing on
vintage champagne in a crystal goblet. There was a soup ladle
for serving the coffee, but unfortunately the chef had not seen fit
to provide any cups. We regretted the disposal of our cardboard
cups at Narbonne – although, by the end of the day they were
very soggy and probably incapable of holding a hot drink.
However, we had a small cup belonging to Helen with a non-
spill top. We brought this into immediate service. Our request
for either sugar or milk was greeted with disdain by the chef and
a very decisive 'non'.

When we had all had a cup of coffee ladled out of the bucket
by the young boy, we heard a tap on our compartment door and
a timid request from the occupants of the adjoining
compartment to borrow our small cup. As our cup made its way
along the coach from compartment to compartment, the chef
began a second march along the platform, this time announcing,
'Du pain. Du pain,' followed by a similar small boy, this one
bearing a large cardboard box full of rolls. We fell on these like

locusts and, duly refreshed, the journey seemed a lot less tedious.

Of course, by the time we reached Calais we had not only missed our night ferry but also the early morning one, and ended up getting a ferry in the mid-afternoon, arriving home well after midnight. Wally and I mutually decided that trains were not for us.

Chapter 14

1976 – Once more to Playa de Aro

After our disastrous choice of resort and mode of travel, we decided that the following year we would go back to our beloved Playa de Aro, travelling by ferry and car. As the Villa Munoz was no longer available, we settled for two adjoining flats in the main street just a short distance from the beach. We took our own six children, three of whom were now teenagers, and Hilary, Jane's friend who had been with us in Llafranch. The journey there was uneventful and we soon settled into the flats. After a few days I became concerned because none of the teenagers showed the least interest in going to the beach. Wally and I would set off soon after breakfast with an assurance from the four girls that they would follow us as soon as they were ready. One o'clock would come and we would return for lunch, to find all four girls sitting on the external staircase at the back of the property. I could not understand this at all. From the front balcony which overlooked the main street, there was at least a view of the sea, but all that could be seen from the back staircase was a building site. Then all became clear to me. Working on the building site were a dozen or more young Spanish men – mostly in their late teens – and our girls, aged sixteen, fifteen and thirteen, found the sight of these young men infinitely more exciting than the beach.

We compromised. The girls would join us every afternoon – this was less a concession on their part than it might have appeared, as I realised that between 1 p.m. and 4 p.m. the young workers were off site for their siesta. The holiday was on the whole very successful. The boys discovered a large outdoor swimming pool at the end of the beach, complete with diving boards, and spent much of their time improving both their swimming and diving.

On our drive down I had noticed a sign that pointed to 'Rennes-le-Chateau', and I made a careful note of exactly where it was, so a visit to this hamlet would be a top priority on our return journey. We found it quite easily, but the church itself was shut. There was a hotel next door where we had a light lunch, and we agreed that it was such an eerie place we would really not want to spend too much time there.

On learning that we would be taking the ferry home from Le Havre, a cousin of mine had suggested that, if time permitted, we might call on her aunts – unknown to me, as they were on her father's side. She had given me the address and, as we made very good time on our drive, I felt I should make every effort to visit them. As we reached the outskirts of the town, I asked a passer-by for directions to Rue de Paris. 'Quelle direction est Rue de Paris, s'il vous plaît?' There followed a long explanation, but the general gist was that we were to turn around and follow signs which would lead us in the right direction. Ten minutes later we were out in the open countryside and Wally said that I had obviously misunderstood. A cyclist was approaching us and once again I asked, 'Quelle direction est Rue de Paris?'. He told us that we were indeed heading in the correct direction. We were puzzled and reluctant to drive further in a direction that was certainly away from, not towards, Le Havre. It was then that I realised that both the pedestrian and the cyclist had thought that I was asking for 'la route de Paris' – the way to Paris. Wally turned the car round and headed back. Once we were back on the outskirts of the town, I took out paper and pen and painstakingly wrote 'Ma tante demeure à 36 Rue de Paris. Pouvez-vous nous donner les directions?' ('My aunt lives at 36 Rue de Paris. Can you please direct us there?') My written French is often intelligible. I ran up to a lady motorist and thrust the paper towards her. She was charming and assured me that she was actually on her way to Rue de Paris and, if we followed her, she would take us right to the door.

The elderly aunts seemed pleased to see us. They ran a small gift shop and, having insisted on giving Helen a doll, we all enjoyed tea with delicious biscuits before leaving to catch our night ferry home.

Chapter 15

1979/80 – Discovering San Antonio (twice)

In 1979, after a three-year gap, we decided once again to head for Spain. This time our friendly travel agent recommended the resort of San Antonio, on the Costa Brava a few miles from Palamós. We booked two apartments in a small, four-block apartment which we felt would be ideal for our party of ten. Sarah, now almost eighteen, and her friend Charlotte were to take the train to Flassa, arriving the day after us, while Katie and her friend Lizzie, John and his friend Andrew, Brendan, Helen, Wally and I would travel in our family estate car.

It was, by our standards, a very successful trip. While we were waiting to board the ferry at Southampton, we met up with another family, also from Cardiff, whose three children were of a similar age to John, Brendan and Helen, and we were very pleased to learn that they also were headed for San Antonio. The drive to our first stop at St Cere was pleasant and totally uneventful. Our old friends, the Bizats, seemed delighted to see us again and we enjoyed a delicious evening meal.

Next morning we set off again, arriving at Palamós to collect the key for our apartment before making the short drive to San Antonio. We found the apartment all we could have hoped for. The larger one on the ground floor had three bedrooms, two for the four girls, and one for the boys. It also had a huge kitchen with dining area. The apartment immediately above was much smaller, with two bedrooms and modest kitchen. Wally, Brendan, Helen and I settled in there with the understanding that all cooking and eating would be in the ground-floor apartment. Maid service was not an option for the apartment.

However, the best part of it all was the location. The apartment, being situated at the very end of the road running alongside the beach with no passing traffic, was only twenty feet from the beach. We were congratulating ourselves on our good fortune when a familiar car drew up outside, and the friends we had met in Southampton climbed out; we learned that they had taken the larger of the two remaining apartments. The children were delighted and wasted no time in getting into swimsuits and heading to the beach. The next day Wally drove to Flassa where, exactly as planned, Sarah and Charlotte arrived on time so that by lunchtime our party was complete. San Antonio suited us perfectly – large enough to offer a choice of food shops and small restaurants – but with none of the noise and traffic associated with larger resorts.

Wally and I enjoyed the adult company of our apartment neighbours and we spent many evenings sitting outside chatting with them once the younger children had gone to bed. The holiday ended all too soon, and we began our trek back home. Once again we stopped in St Cere, enjoying our meal and excellent accommodation. When we had made our booking for the overnight ferry for our return, we found that, as all the cabins had been reserved, we were offered recliner seats in the quiet lounge. We found these and settled down to try to sleep –

at least, Wally, the girls and I made tried to sleep, but the boys had other plans. Having already set their sights on the array of fruit machines in the main lounge, they had protested at being hauled off to the quiet lounge. Wally fell asleep quite quickly, exhausted after another day of driving. I eventually drifted off into a fitful sleep but, waking a short while later, realised that the boys were no longer with us. It did not take long to work out that they were twenty yards away in the main lounge playing on the fruit machines. I found them, chivvied them back and once again attempted to sleep.

During the night the boys displayed determination of heroic proportions. Every time I dozed off, up they got, heading straight to the machines and, on waking a short while later, up I got to chase them back. I didn't mind them playing the machines and using their own pocket money, but I had noticed that the lounge was full of fellow passengers who, unable to get reservations for even reclining seats, were attempting to stretch out for a sleep in the main lounge. The machines were not particularly noisy, except when making a modest cash pay-out, but the same could not be said for the boys. I was glad when dawn came and we sighted Southampton.

However, feeling that the holiday had been a great success, we decided to book again for the following year, 1980, and our Cardiff friends also decided to book for the same two weeks. We were unable to book the same apartment but, as our party was now reducing in size, we settled for one a little further along towards the town but still only twenty feet from the beach. By this time Sarah and Katie had both decided to go their own ways as far as holidays were concerned, so our party was made up of me, Wally, John and his friends Andrew and Patrick, Brendan and Helen.

Unfortunately, the success of the previous year's holiday lulled us into a sense of false security as far as travelling was concerned. By now a number of our friends had taken to making the journey to Spain by car and several of them had expressed surprise that we should stop overnight in France whereas they had travelled straight through from the ferry direct to Spain. Assured by them of the excellence of French motorways, we decided to break with our tradition of overnight sailing by taking a day ferry and driving through France during the night.

I can only assume that our friends recommending this particular journey either had stronger nerves, fewer children or better vehicles – possibly all three – because, of all the journeys which we had made, this one was – for me – the most traumatic. In 1980, juggernauts were virtually unknown on British roads and so we were quite unprepared for the size of the vehicles which we encountered on our journey through France. The box-type trailers were often 50 feet long and, even more worryingly, two were sometimes linked together. Furthermore, all these units were outlined – sides and back – with small electric lightbulbs. The reason for this never became clear – could it have been a safety measure or an advertising ploy? Whatever the reason, the result – as they thundered past us on the passenger side of our car – was like being overtaken by a mobile fairground.

Wally has never been a speed merchant, especially at night, but it soon became evident that the other motorway drivers had no concept of the speed limit and were not at all happy with our cruising at a mere 60 miles per hour. I freely admit that I was terrified and, when we finally reached a service station near Lyon at 5 a.m., we stopped for breakfast and I phoned Sarah and Katie at home to tell them where they could find our wills – so certain was I that they would surely be in need of them over the next few hours. Admittedly, it was 4 a.m. British time, which may account for this information being received with rather less concern than might have been expressed. I felt that, 'What? Yeah. OK,' did not really convey the alarm and sorrow which might have been expected on receiving the news of our imminent demise.

Once breakfast was over, we returned to our car and found that now the dawn had broken driving was a lot easier – if only because the lights on the juggernauts were no longer a feature, and also as we drew nearer to Spain the heavy traffic lessened considerably. Even so, we did not arrive at Palamós to collect our key until 3 p.m. – also collecting the key for our Cardiff friends as they were not due to arrive until much later (and eventually arrived, totally exhausted, at 11.30 p.m.). The very next day I scoured my French motorists' handbook and map of France and began planning an alternative – motorway-free – route home. I found a small hotel which had rooms available for the night before our ferry booking. This meant that we would leave San Antonio a day earlier than originally planned, but I felt that the sacrifice of one day's holiday was a small price to pay for thirty or possibly forty years of life.

Unfortunately our funds were unexpectedly depleted on our first day. Helen, aged eight, had run enthusiastically out onto the balcony of our apartment, crashing through the glass door leading from the sitting room to the balcony, so we had to pay for both the new glass and the glazier's time. I suspect that Helen, familiar with the state of our glass doors and windows at home, had simply failed to appreciate that finger marks, paw marks and ball marks are not an intrinsic feature of glass – which can appear completely clear – and she had assumed that the door was open. This meant that we ate out on very few occasions that holiday.

Chapter 16

1981 – San Antonio and the Royal Wedding

Still filled with enthusiasm for San Antonio, we decided to book again for 1981, as did our Cardiff friends. This time, as Sarah and her friend Jackie had agreed to join us, we booked the two apartments at the end of the beach which we had taken in 1979. The older girls travelled by train, with the rest of our party going by car: Wally, Helen and I, John and his friend Andrew, and Brendan and his friend Peter. We stayed very firmly on the small roads, making an overnight stop in France. All went well until we arrived at our agent's office in Palamós to collect the key. For some inexplicable reason our car, which up until that moment had behaved impeccably, refused to move another inch. San Antonio was about five miles away by road but, as we knew from our previous holidays, only a mile across the beach. Leaving Wally to sort out the problem of the car, we unloaded our more essential items and began the trek across the sands. As we drew near to the beach – and our apartment was at the Palamós end of the beach – we realised that our arrival was causing something of a stir. Our Cardiff friends – who this year had opted to fly – were already there, staring in amazement as all six of us, dragging our cases behind us, appeared, looking more like a party of refugees than a group of British holidaymakers. Wally arrived about an hour later. The problem with the car had proved a minor one and he was able to collect Sarah and Jackie from the station the next morning.

As 1981 was the year of Prince Charles and Lady Diana Spencer's wedding, I was determined that we should not miss out on any of the celebrations which we would have enjoyed had we been at home. Accordingly, I packed an appropriate number of disposable cups, plates and napkins emblazoned with photographs of the royal couple for use at the party we intended to have on the evening of the wedding. Anxious not to miss seeing the event on television, we soon discovered that almost every bar in the town was going to show it. We chose one near our apartment, settling ourselves in a good position for viewing. Of course, the commentary was in Spanish but, to our amazement, we learned that the mother-in-law of the bar owner was a devotee of all matters royal, even possessing an encyclopaedic knowledge not only of the British royal family but also of the Spanish, Greek, Dutch, Belgian royal families, and even smaller or long-defunct monarchies. The moment any guest with the remotest royal connection appeared on the screen, she would launch into a biography along the lines of 'third cousin four times removed'. Her son-in-law kindly translated this into English for our benefit – by which time a new guest would be making an entrance. I felt she would have been enormously useful to the BBC, and her talent was quite wasted in San Antonio.

Once the televised wedding was over, we began to prepare for the evening's entertainment. As our apartment was right at the end of the road, with no through traffic, it was easy to set up a street party. Our Cardiff friends were only too happy to celebrate with us and, to our surprise, we were approached by a Greek family staying in a nearby apartment, and a Spanish couple who lived just behind, who also asked if they could join in. As dusk fell, twenty-four of us sat down to a meal of cold meats, cheese, salads and copious amounts of wine. Two elderly Dutch ladies came along but, while wishing us well, felt that their age might put a damper on our celebrations. However, they asked if they could have the small Union Jacks from our table when the party was over. They both had memories of the British Forces' efforts on their behalf in 1944.

The night wore on, complete with lots of music from our tape recorder: 'I wonder what the king is doing tonight' from Camelot played over and over and, of course, a selection of Beatles favourites. Finally, at around 1 a.m. somebody suggested that to have a really British ending to the night we should all dance the Conga along the street. We lined up and set off. About four hundred yards along, we came to a small hotel largely occupied by a group of Scottish holidaymakers who, like us, had been marking the royal occasion. On learning that we came from Wales, they insisted that we sing them something in Welsh. The Welsh are renowned for the excellence of their singing – a reputation lost the moment that any member of my family utters a note. However, buoyed up by the spirit of the occasion – not to mention the wine – we agreed.

After a hasty consultation we decided to sing 'Sospan fach', which is usually sung at rugby matches and has words that were simple enough for us to remember. Whether we would have remembered more than the first two lines will never be known, because within moments of our starting to sing we heard the sound of sirens and fast-approaching cars. Now, the father of our Cardiff friends was at that time a high-ranking official in the South Wales police force. It must have taken him all of ten seconds to sum up the situation and decide on his plan of action. He leaped over the wall of the house next to the small hotel, raced through its garden and scaled the garden wall at the end, gaining access to the street behind, from where he was able to make his way back unhindered to his family's apartment.

Meanwhile, the rest of our party stood like statues while three police cars, with sirens blaring and blue lights flashing, drew up alongside us. From each of the cars leaped three police officers, all with guns holstered at their side. They spoke to us in rapid Spanish – none of which we could truly understand – but the general gist was that we were disturbing the peace of San Antonio so that, unless we stopped at once and returned to our apartments, retribution would follow. We readily agreed to leave and, whispering our 'goodnights' to our new Scottish friends, wound our way back up the road to our apartment. On reflection, when I considered the expressions on the faces of the wife and three children of our police officer friend, I could not but wonder if a night spent in the local Spanish jail may not have been a preferable alternative to confronting them when they returned to find him in their apartment! A few days later our holiday was over and we began our homeward trek.

Still filled with a desire to add some historical or cultural interest to our journeys, before leaving home we had made a reservation for the night before our ferry departure in a hotel within a short drive of Mont St Michel. This is a small rocky islet between Normandy and Brittany, ninety-four miles from Le Havre. Its main feature is a Benedictine abbey dedicated to St Michael, the archangel, and it is of architectural and religious importance, dating back to the eleventh century. I cannot say that this was fully or even remotely appreciated by the boys. While Wally, Helen and I made the 900-step climb to the church at the top, the boys settled at a cafe at street level and ordered themselves plates of chips.

Remembering the difficulty I had had in trying to keep the boys away from the fruit machines when we didn't have overnight cabins, we had made sure that we booked in plenty of time to get two four-berth cabins for our return. Wally, Helen and I were in one on the second deck, while the boys were all in one on the fifth deck. The three of us fell asleep very quickly, but we were abruptly woken by a knocking on our door. Wally got up to open it and John marched in and threw himself onto the spare bunk, muttering, 'I'm not staying down there, it's full of men in gold braid.' This completely mystified us and Wally, with John in tow, set off to investigate.

Sure enough, if not 'full of men in gold braid', there were certainly two men there both wearing gold-braided uniforms – one was the purser and the other was the chief engineer. In a few short questions, Wally had managed to piece together the story. The cabin was close to the engine room and Brendan – then twelve – had decided that it was too noisy for him to sleep there and had gone to find the purser to complain and request another cabin, on the grounds that 'he had paid to sleep on the boat and the noise was preventing this'. The purser accompanied him back to the cabin and tried to say a few comforting words, but Brendan was not to be deterred and suggested that the noise could be indicative of a fault in the engines and he felt that the ship's engineer should be called.

Customer satisfaction must have been the top priority on this ship as the purser went away and returned with the ship's engineer, similarly attired in gold-braided uniform. It was at this point that John left for our cabin. Wally, faced with these two officers, apologised on Brendan's behalf and ordered all four boys to get into their bunks and go to sleep. The next morning, when we were preparing to leave the ship, I tried to distance myself from Brendan as we passed the purser, so embarrassed was I, but Brendan had no such qualms and, placing himself next to me, called out a cheery 'goodbye' to him as we left. The purser must have felt relief as we made our way to the car deck, out of his sight and his duty of care.

Chapter 17

1984 – To Minorca by plane

Holidays did not enter into our plans for the next two years as we were fully occupied with the illness and subsequent death of my mother, who was living with us. However, in 1984 I saw a holiday advertised which offered excellent self-catering accommodation with a large swimming pool attached to the apartment block and within two hundred yards of a sandy beach. More importantly, it was at an amazingly reasonable cost.

There was one small problem. It involved flying to Minorca which, I suspected, would not appeal to my husband. However, I felt that, since it offered such good value, Wally could surely be persuaded to set aside his antipathy to flying so that the two of us and twelve-year-old Helen could enjoy two weeks of sunshine. He allowed himself to be persuaded and, as in 1964 and 1967, we flew from our local airport. It was seventeen years since Wally had last flown, but it soon became evident that the passing of the years had done nothing to erase his memory of our trip in 1964. Shortly after take-off, he managed to spill the entire contents of his courtesy glass of orange juice all over my pale blue linen dress, drenching it from neck to hem. I sat there for the next two hours while the orange juice soaked through to my skin. I received some very strange looks from fellow passengers and airport officials as we made our way through baggage collection and Customs, but at last we were in a taxi taking us to our resort and our apartment. It was all I had hoped for, and we settled down to enjoying the next two weeks.

We loved Minorca. We went by local bus to other resorts and into Mahon itself on a few occasions and, on one of these visits, I saw a sign advertising day-long cruises around the island, one of which offered a stopover on a beach accessible only by boat, with a barbecue lunch included. We decided to take advantage of this and the next day left early by bus to Mahon and then made our way to the boat stage. Several queues had already begun to form, but I noticed that some were lining up for half-day cruises or trips to a specific resort. We joined the queue that clearly indicated (in Spanish) that it was the whole day cruise with barbecue included. It probably indicated something else, but I either did not trouble to read it or failed to understand what it said. Within five minutes of setting off, our tour guide began to tell us something of the sights we could now see from the boat. She spoke in German, and we sat patiently waiting for her to repeat it in English. We sailed on and, faced with a new sight, once again she began to give out the information in German and once again we waited in vain for the English explanation. We then tuned our ears to conversations among our fellow passengers and the truth dawned upon us – they were all speaking in German. We had managed to join the tour designed for German tourists instead of the one alongside it for English-speaking visitors. That, of course, was what the latter part of the sign had indicated, but which I had failed to read.

Our cruise continued and it was a little frustrating not to be able to understand what our guide was saying about the various buildings, or why expressions of surprise or sorrow were being expressed by our fellow passengers listening to her. After about forty-five minutes we passed a very pretty and totally deserted beach, and our guide broke into a long spiel in German. Whatever she said was greeted with loud guffaws of laughter and a few remarks from some of the passengers, followed by more laughter. We could not understand what had caused this mirth, and assumed that she had told them a joke in German. Five minutes later the boat turned in towards the next small cove, and pulled up onto the beach.

The passengers began to get off. As we were leaving I told our guide that we were British and had obviously joined the wrong tour. 'Och, hen,' she replied, 'I'm from Glasgow myself.' She was very friendly and assured us that on our return journey she would sit next to us and give us the information about the various sights. Meanwhile, her two young male assistants had unloaded all the equipment and food from the boat and had begun to set up the barbecue. In order to keep the children amused while waiting for the food to be cooked, she organised a sandcastle competition. Helen, at twelve, felt she might be a bit too old for this, but as two German boys who seemed a year or two older had already begun constructing theirs, she thought she may as well join in.

She built quite a creditable castle and then thought she would add a final touch. She had brought with her a small sketchpad and packet of crayons and, with these, she drew and coloured a very authentic-looking Union Jack. She found a small stick on the beach and, attaching the flag, she placed it carefully on top of her castle. Our tour guide began to judge the castles. Now, I do not know whether our being British played any part in her decision to award the first prize to Helen – a packet of boiled sweets – but it certainly caused a few surly looks and muttered comments from some of the other contestants, particularly the two older boys whose construction, in their opinion, was vastly superior to hers. I also had the feeling that the display of the Union Jack may have given rise to concern that British colonialism was about to put out a shoot on this deserted beach in Minorca.

We began our lunch, which was excellent and well-cooked and we all enjoyed it. Then, once it was cleared away, our guide announced – in German and in English – that there was now going to be a limbo-dancing contest. Wally was horrified. He is a tall man and he simply could not conceive of the idea of dancing under a pole in front of so many strangers so, while a number of the others began to vie with each other over who would go first, we gathered up our towels and began to quietly make our way to the back of the beach where a small path wound up to the cliff at the top. We walked along a narrow pathway and within a few hundred yards had found another small deserted cove with a path leading down to it. Taking this route to the beach, we laid out our towels and stretched out in the sun. After about twenty minutes, we decided to go for a swim.

We had been in the sea for about five minutes when a boat turned into the cove and pulled up to the beach. About twenty people got off – all stark naked. They set about laying towels on the sand and stretched out in the sun. The three of us, still in the sea, did not know what we should do. It was now obvious that this beach was what had caused the laughter on the boat – it was a nudist beach and I had a strong suspicion that people wearing clothes would not be made welcome, possibly even fined. We stayed in the sea, trying very hard to only show our heads above the water. There was something farcical in the fact that we felt too embarrassed to come out of the sea because we were wearing swimsuits. Eventually all the sunbathers decided that they would go for a swim and, as soon as they were safely in the sea, we made a quick dash onto the beach, gathered up our towels and ran up the path at the back of the beach. We made our way back to the barbecue beach, where we were glad to see that the limbo-dancing contest had now ended and prizes were being given out. It was time to get back into the boat and head back to Mahon. Our guide was as good as her word and explained all the sights to us – including the nudist beach – with which we were now all too familiar.

Our holiday came to an end and all too soon Wally had to face the ordeal of the flight home. His nerves had not improved, and in his anxious state he dropped his glasses and smashed one lens. His glasses were of a particularly strong and expensive prescription and the cost of their replacement, coupled with my ruined dress, made me wonder if financially the holiday had been quite such a good bargain, although in terms of enjoyment it could not have been faulted.

Chapter 18

1988 – To Leucate by train

For a variety of reasons, it was 1988 before we took another holiday. By now Sarah was married, Katie, John and Brendan were all living in London, and only Helen remained at home. As our helpful travel agent had now retired, we decided to research our holiday ourselves. We selected Port Leucate in southern France and decided to travel there by train. Helen invited her friend, Bridget, to join us and we booked an overnight sleeper from Paris to Leucate. Of course, when we had travelled by train before, the size of our party ensured that we had not needed to share our sleeping accommodation with strangers. Now we found ourselves sharing with an elderly Frenchman and his young grandson. Neither of them spoke any English but, with nods and smiles, we happily settled in. As the train moved off, the Frenchman brought out his supper. This consisted of rolls filled – I am sure – with neat garlic. The smell was overpowering and completely destroyed any vestige of flavour that may have lurked in our own rather boring cheese sandwiches. On the pretext of suffering from the heat, I managed to open the window, but as night fell and we all climbed into our sleeping berths, the Frenchman indicated that he would like to close the window against the cold night air. As he had eaten his meal, I did not see this as a problem. However, once sleep overtook him, he began to snore. The sound itself was not particularly disturbing, but every time a snore emitted from his mouth, so did the overpowering smell of garlic. Fortunately, he was not travelling as far as Leucate and left the train soon after 7 a.m. We carried on for a further two hours until finally the train stopped at a station which boldly stated on a large sign that we were at 'Leucate'.

We all got off and pulled our cases on to the platform. Then we looked around. We were the only passengers to get off at this stop, and the station itself was absolutely desolate. The scene from *Butch Cassidy and the Sundance Kid* where Butch, Sundance and Etta arrive by train at a station in Bolivia expecting to find affluence and activity, but find only a tethered llama, eight pigs and four piglets rooting around, came into my mind. We, however, had nothing – not even the piglets and certainly not the llama. The station had two platforms serving the two lines. Looking immediately behind us we could see nothing but rows and rows of grapevines stretching into infinity. Looking across the lines to the other platform and beyond it, again there was nothing but grapevines. Up the line and down the line – wherever we looked, we saw nothing else. Picturesque, perhaps, but where were the sparkling sea and sandy beach? And, even more importantly, how on earth were we to leave the station? I could see no sign of a road anywhere. Then I caught sight of a piece of paper fluttering from a telegraph pole on the opposite platform and on it I could just make out the word 'TAXI'. I turned to Helen. 'Go over and see what else it says.'

She demurred for a moment but, having spent the last twenty years being the sole translator and interpreter, I felt the time had come to pass this particular baton on to Helen. She was by now sixteen and something of a linguist. Furthermore, she had just completed her French O-level with the intention of carrying on with it at A-level. She obligingly jumped down onto the railway line, ran across and hauled herself up onto the opposite platform, where she went to examine the notice. She called to tell us that there was a telephone fixed to the other side of the pole and a notice giving the (free) number to ring for a taxi. I told her to go ahead, and the three of us began to make our way across to her.

We scrambled down from the platform and pulled our cases after us. After dragging them across the two sets of lines, we lugged both ourselves and our cases up on to the other platform. I could see no sign of a road, and could not imagine where the taxi would arrive. Then Helen pointed out that, thirty feet directly below us, there was indeed a road and there was even access to it – several flights of steep narrow concrete steps winding around and eventually reaching road level. We began our descent. It was probably quite difficult even without any baggage – with our cases, it was positively hazardous. We eventually reached the road and after a surprisingly short time a taxi duly appeared.

As we drove along, the scenery did not change. There was nothing but grapevines on both sides. After five or six miles, I began to panic. Why on earth had I elected to come to this particular resort? Even if we had been interested in the grape harvest, as far as I could see, the grapes were a good two months away from being ripe enough to pick. After another few miles, we reached the brow of a small incline and there, ahead of us, we could see the sea, sparkling in the sunshine. The relief I felt was immeasurable. Port Leucate was a modern resort built on an inlet and was very popular with boat-owners. Our apartment was all we could have wanted, with lovely views of the marina and a very short walk from a quiet and sandy beach with good swimming. After we had been there for a couple of days, we learned that there were four Leucates! There was Port Leucate, where we were staying. There was Leucate Plage on the Mediterranean, which was the site of a lighthouse for that stretch of coast. There was the original town of Leucate, which had shops and amenities, and, finally, there was the 'there is absolutely nothing here except an unmanned railway station' Leucate – which is where we had arrived. We ventured into the original Leucate by bus on a couple of occasions but we were generally content to stay in Port Leucate.

We also learned that most visitors to Port Leucate either arrived by car, private boat, or flew in to Perpignan Airport, which was about fifteen miles away. For visitors to arrive by train was practically unknown. Bearing this in mind, I decided that when we left I would book a taxi to take us to the station to allow us at least half an hour on the platform before the train was due. I suspected that the train service around Leucate may operate along similar lines to buses in rural Britain (that is, they would stop if a passenger wished to get off or if there was someone standing at the bus stop, with arm outstretched, preferably waving some brightly coloured object and possibly stepping a pace or two into the road itself). I felt it was imperative that we made ourselves as visible as possible on the platform – all four of us with cases to the fore, waving and gesturing, to leave no doubt in the driver's mind that we wanted to get on the train. The ploy worked, and soon we were all on board and headed for home. This time we did not have to share our sleeping accommodation with anyone else, and the journey was pleasant and unremarkable.

Chapter 19

1988–1998 – North Wales and flight mishaps

Freed now from the need for sea, sand and sun for the children, Wally and I spent the next few years mainly travelling in Britain – either in the company of friends or by ourselves –from Cornwall to Scotland, from West Wales to East Anglia, mostly by car but occasionally by train. None of these holidays offered us any real challenge – both born and bred in Britain, neither the language nor the road signs presented us with any difficulty. On reflection, however, this is not entirely true. In 1988 we took a tour around north Wales. Welsh is widely spoken in north Wales, but in south-east Wales – where we lived – it was rarely spoken, and I had very little knowledge of it. Before we left on that holiday our very good friends Margot and Philip had told me they were hoping to buy a small guest house in some tourist location, and asked me if I would look out for anything that could be suitable. As we drove around the beautiful countryside,

I noticed a number of signs all bearing the agent's name, 'AR WERTH', but never, in any of the small towns, did I see an office for this agent. As the afternoon drew to a close, I mentioned this fact to Wally. He stared at me; he could not believe I was serious. 'Ar werth,' he explained, means, 'for sale' in Welsh. So that accounted for the abundance of signs and absence of offices. In the end, our friends bought a guest house in Scotland.

I also travelled quite extensively on my own during the 1990s, mostly by air and mostly, although not entirely, without incident. In 1989 I was paying a four-week visit to the USA and Canada, catching up, thirty-one years on, with my American college friends and Canadian cousins. I was flying from Toronto to Columbus, Ohio on a flight that was scheduled to make a one-hour stopover in Washington, DC before continuing on to Miami.

Having checked in my main bags, I was holding my cabin bag which contained my passport, money, make-up, book and all the other bits and pieces I thought I might require on the flight. I inadvertently placed this on a conveyor belt which I took to be the X-ray machine for checking hand luggage and, to my horror, it disappeared through a curtain and into the hold of the plane. I was fraught. I raced over to the check-in desk and explained the problem to the attendant, pointing out that this bag was not tagged. It was shortly after the Lockerbie disaster of December 1988, and airlines were particularly aware of the danger of carrying any piece of luggage not clearly belonging to a passenger on board the flight. The attendant telephoned through to the baggage handlers and I was assured that my bag would soon appear on the carousel. I was to go over and wait for it.

The carousel was a good hundred yards away, but I raced to it and stood patiently by. After thirty-five minutes I could hear my flight being called, so I ran back to the check-in desk, only to be told that the flight could not possibly leave until I had been reunited with my bag. Back I went to the carousel. By now, not only was my flight number being called, but I was also being called by name. There seemed to have been a lack of communication between the check-in desk, the baggage handlers and the Immigration department, the latter being responsible for all passengers heading to the USA. I waited and waited. Finally my dark green cabin bag appeared on the carousel – a small and isolated object travelling slowly towards me. I grabbed it up and ran the hundred yards to Immigration.

A large queue of passengers waiting for later planes stood ahead of me. I ignored them all, leading to some quite aggressive remarks from a large American man whose flight, I noticed, was not due to take off for a further thirty minutes. Frostily I informed him that unless I went through Immigration immediately he would be lucky if his plane left that day – let alone within the next thirty minutes. The Immigration officer greeted me with some relief. 'The missing Mrs Laing,' he said. Then, having checked my passport, he added – in a tone not to brook any argument – 'RUN!' And run I did.

The stewardess met me with a smile and guided me to my seat. Then came the announcement: 'Due to the delay in take-off time, it will not be possible for passengers bound for Miami to leave the plane at Washington.' I was so embarrassed and felt sorry for all the passengers who had been looking forward to an hour browsing the duty-free shops or using the well-appointed toilet facilities at Washington Airport. I slouched down in my seat and did not even raise my head to take up the offer of free orange juice and peanuts.

My other travel trauma occurred in 1998 when, planning to fly to Paris, I inadvertently boarded a plane bound for Palma. This, I stress, was not my fault. I had booked a flight from our local airport for a Friday evening to spend the weekend with Helen who was teaching English in a language school there. Brendan had driven me to the airport in plenty of time and I had checked in. I only had hand luggage for this short visit. I made my way to the gate shown on the flight departures board, and sat down to wait until we were called to the plane. There was a party of five or six schoolgirls also waiting at this gate. After fifteen minutes, a woman came along and gathered them up and herded them away. I took no notice of this – I didn't know where they were going and they were of no interest to me.

Shortly after this, an airline official beckoned the rest of us to make our way to the plane. As we left the terminal building to cross the tarmac another official examined our boarding cards. I noticed a small plane standing nearby, but I was waved to a much larger one further away. I climbed up the steps and again presented my card to the steward, who nodded and pointed me up the aisle. I was rather surprised to find that the seat which had been allocated to me was occupied, and I returned to the steward to query this – again producing my boarding card. He looked around the plane and told me to sit where I could find a seat. This was not difficult, as the plane was only about three-quarters full, but I did find it a little strange.

The plane began to taxi up the runway and the pilot made his usual announcement: 'Welcome aboard this flight to Palma.' I sat up and raised my hand. I began to speak, but it was too late – the recorded announcement regarding all the safety features had already begun, and the stewards and stewardesses were pointing out the directions to the emergency exits, following this with a demonstration of how to put on life jackets in the event of an emergency. By the time this had ended and the cabin was silent, we had reached the end of the runway and the pilot was beginning to rev up the engines for take-off. In that moment of silence I spoke. 'But I'm going to Paris.' Nothing I had ever said before or since has produced such a dramatic effect. Three stewards rushed towards me and all three examined my boarding card. I produced the duplicate copy of my airline ticket as further evidence. The pilot was informed, and stopped revving the engines. A telephone call was made to the terminal building and then, slowly but inexorably, the plane was turned around and began its ponderous journey back to the terminal, where the cabin door was opened, the steps were wheeled across the tarmac and I stepped from the plane. I felt a great deal of sympathy for the passengers still on board (especially, as I later learned, that, due to the delay in departure from this airport, they missed their slot at their next stop; their last pick-up point in the UK before carrying on to Palma. It led to a three-hour delay in their time of arrival).

However, my own problems were just beginning. While I was sitting on the plane listening to the endless safety announcements, my flight to Paris had been called and my name had been called repeatedly throughout the building. I, of course, was ignorant of this. Had I had baggage checked in, the plane could not have left without me – at least until those items of baggage had been removed from the hold. However, having only hand luggage, the airline officials assumed that I had changed my mind about the journey and were happy for the plane to take off without me. The schoolgirls who had been gathered up had been escorted to the small plane bound for Paris by an airline official. Unfortunately, she had not been informed of my booking on that same flight. Back at the check-in desk, I asked about the next flight to Paris. This was on Sunday morning – which was of little use to me, wanting to spend the weekend with Helen. However, the British Airways assistant told me that there was a flight from Bristol Airport the next morning at 7.30 a.m. and they could book me on to that. I accepted this offer and considered how to make my way to Bristol, which was about sixty miles away. This was, of course, when mobile phones were rare and I certainly did not have one. I was very concerned for Helen, who had planned to meet me at Charles de Gaulle Airport, and I begged the British Airways assistant to telephone their Paris desk and leave a message for her, explaining what had happened and asking her to meet me the following morning.

Further help was offered by this assistant, who told me that a bus which would take me back to my home town, Cardiff, was due within the next few minutes, so I left the terminal in haste and within a very few minutes I was on my way back home. As we pulled into Cardiff's main bus terminal I spotted a bus marked 'Bristol', and as I ran to ask what time it was due to leave, the driver turned on his engine and succinctly informed me, 'Now'. I jumped on and, an hour later, arrived in Bristol, where the driver directed me to a hotel a short walk from the bus station. They had a single room and I thankfully booked myself into it. By now it was 9.30 p.m. and I should have arrived in Paris at 7 p.m. As soon as I got into my bedroom, I telephoned home. Everyone there was frantic. Helen had arrived at Charles de Gaulle Airport to meet me, and not only was there no mother on the flight, there was no message about what had happened to me either. Brendan protested that he had definitely delivered me to the airport, and enquiries there confirmed that I had checked in, but as to what had happened afterwards, no one apparently knew. This gave rise to wild speculation on the part of my family – had I developed amnesia? Could I be wandering aimlessly around the airport? Had I gone off on some mysterious trip of my own to heaven only knew where? I think they all discounted my abduction by aliens.

I calmed them down and begged them to telephone Helen immediately. Surprisingly, I slept well and booked a taxi to get me to the airport in good time. The flight was straightforward; Helen met me and we enjoyed a lovely weekend together. When I returned home, I wrote to both British Airways and the Airport Authority requesting compensation. Two planes should never leave from the same gate at approximately the same time – which was what had happened. The smaller plane, which I had noticed but had been waved past, was in fact the plane to Paris. To prove that I was the innocent party in this fiasco, I am happy to say that within two weeks I received a cheque from British Airways covering all my expenses – including my flight from

Bristol, my bus fares, hotel bill, taxi fare, even Helen's fare for her abortive journey from the centre of Paris to Charles de Gaulle Airport on the Friday evening. I felt I had been totally exonerated.

Chapter 20

1998 – To Poland and back

Of course, compared with some of the journeys we had taken with the children, these incidents were minor and we had begun to believe that our days of travel trials and tribulations were behind us. How misplaced was our optimism. In early 1999 we received an invitation from our very good friends, Margot and Philip, to attend their son's wedding, who was marrying a girl from Poland in Warsaw in June. This would give Wally a challenge – something he had sorely missed since we no longer took holidays in Spain. All the other British guests went off to their local travel agent and booked themselves on flights from Heathrow or Gatwick direct to Warsaw. There was nothing so simple for us. Wally equipped himself with maps of Western Europe and Eastern Europe and the Times atlas of the world and began to plot our itinerary.

Late 1994 had seen the opening of the Channel Tunnel and the Eurostar train service from London to both Paris and Brussels. Having already used this service once on a visit to

Paris, I felt it offered an excellent way of reaching Warsaw with minimum inconvenience. Studying the maps, we thought that to travel that distance without seeing a little more of Eastern Europe would be a wasted chance, and so Wally planned a route whereby we would travel by train to London from where we would take the Eurostar to Brussels. Then we would pick up a connection to Cologne, finishing on an overnight sleeper train to Prague. After spending a day in Prague, we would complete our journey via a sleeper train to Warsaw.

The difficulty arose when we set about booking tickets for this trip. The first part was easy – our local rail travel centre was more than happy to sell me the tickets for our journey to London, but told me that all other stages of the journey would have to be made by contacting the individual train companies. This was, of course, before booking by internet was possible. Mercifully, for the sake of our phone bill, all the train companies had offices in London.

The Eurostar booking was made with surprising efficiency, as was the booking to Cologne. However, when it came to making our reservations on the German train from Cologne to Prague, I ran into difficulties as the timetable relating to our period of travel was not yet available. Over the next six weeks I made innumerable phone calls before I was able to make our booking to Prague. Once we had this, I felt able to turn my attention to the final stage – from Prague to Warsaw overnight, with a return from Warsaw direct to Cologne – again overnight.

It was when I phoned Polish Rail in London that I faced a problem. There was no difficulty in booking the tickets, but when I requested a sleeping compartment for me and my husband I was greeted with what I could only assume to be a shocked silence. Then a stern voice informed me in no uncertain tone that, 'There are no mixed sleepinks on Polish trains.' I protested that we had been married for forty years, but the voice on the phone merely reiterated that, 'There are no mixed sleepinks on Polish trains.' I felt that to break through this barrier would probably require intervention by the Foreign Office, or perhaps the United Nations, so I gave up and accepted the peculiarities of Polish rail sleeping arrangements.

The tickets and sleeping car vouchers arrived and I noted that we had over a two-hour wait in Cologne – an ideal opportunity to sample some German food, particularly as we had never visited Germany before. Being completely ignorant of restaurant prices in Germany, I decided to take £60 in Deutschmarks which I hoped would be sufficient to enable us to enjoy a good meal in a Cologne restaurant.

The journey to London passed without a hitch and we arrived in Brussels on the Eurostar at the precise time advertised. Once there, we asked which was the platform for the train to Cologne, and were told that it was Platform 5. It was not that far from the Eurostar's arrival platform to Platform 5, but we had with us two suitcases and a large, extremely cumbersome, hat-box. Although our stay was not going to be a long one, we had to pack a suit for Wally and a wedding outfit for me and, as we were planning to have a few days sightseeing, clothes suitable for walking around – possibly in the rain. It was the hat-box that caused the greatest inconvenience. It was octagonal in shape and almost twenty-four inches wide, and one or other of the eight corners bumped my legs at every step. We made our way to a long flight of steps leading to Platform 5 and were reassured to see a large sign announcing that the next train would be going to Cologne. Twenty minutes passed, as did the time of departure. Suddenly a diminutive female official appeared. 'Is anyone going to Cologne?' she called out in perfect English. Wally and I owned up at once, as did a young American woman standing near us. 'Then you should be on Platform 15,' she shouted accusingly. We began an apologetic murmur about being informed that Platform 5 was correct, but the American woman started expressing her opinion of both Belgian and German railways in terms and language that made me fear for our NATO relationship.

As fast as we could, we went back down the stairs and towards Platform 15. It was not an especially long distance, but the hat-box did not help. We climbed up the stairs to Platform 15. The train was in, and we got on board and found our seats. The train left the station. Ten minutes into our journey, the train halted and an announcement was made in three languages informing us that, due to an accident further along the line, there would be an hour's delay to our journey. This, together with the half-hour delay in leaving Brussels, meant that our time in Cologne had been reduced to less than one hour, and there seemed no possibility of leaving the station and finding a restaurant. However, we still had hopes of enjoying a meal at a restaurant within the station, and consoled ourselves with this thought as we gazed at the unimpressive scenery on the outskirts of Brussels.

We reached Cologne, and disembarked. I have seldom seen such a depressing station. I believe it was undergoing a major refurbishment, part of which had necessitated removing the roof. To add to our misery, it was raining quite heavily.

We asked where we could find the restaurant, and were eventually directed to the only source of food and drink in the entire station. It was a small kiosk selling German sausages, beer and coffee. I like English sausages, but these sausages could – in size, shape and texture – have substituted for a policeman's truncheon of earlier times, and I decided that a coffee would be quite sufficient. As we sat forlornly under a flimsy plastic awning, clutching beer and coffee, I took comfort from the thought that, of the £60 reserved for our meal, £57.30 still remained.

When our train arrived – on time – all was forgiven. Our sleeping compartment was superb – well-equipped with a plentiful supply of mineral water and orange juice, and a most helpful steward who told us he would fetch us any other drinks and prepare our beds when required. As our journey was to take us along the Rhine and as we still had two hours of daylight left, we asked him to leave the seats in position until night fell. As promised, our steward came when called and, with a few deft moves, transformed our seats into two comfortable bunk beds with mattresses, pillows, sheets, blankets and bedside lights. Finally he offered to keep our passports, to save us being disturbed going over the Czech border in the night.

When morning came, he woke us and, again with a seemingly magic touch, converted our beds back into a seat, this time managing to produce a small table in the middle on which he placed our breakfast, which consisted of orange juice, yoghurts, croissants and rolls with a plentiful supply of freshly brewed coffee. We arrived at Prague station on time and, leaving our cases and hat-box in the luggage office, went off to explore the city's attractions.

Having only one day there, we decided that the best way to start our exploration would be to take a sightseeing tour bus. We were directed to its main departure point where we bought our tickets for the first tour of the day. Prague is an incredibly beautiful city, filled with many buildings of historic and architectural interest, and therefore we were more than a little surprised to find that our first stop was opposite a quite modestly-sized Tesco store. This was pointed out to us with great pride. I was bemused. I could not imagine myself – or, indeed, anyone in Britain – regarding a Tesco store as a major tourist attraction, certainly not one you would pay good money to view. Once we had all made appropriate appreciative noises, the bus moved on to a magnificent cathedral and a variety of other beautiful churches and palaces. In the afternoon we decided to take a trip along the Vltava River. The views were beautiful, but unfortunately it began to rain and I, trying to preserve my hairstyle for the wedding, went below deck, while Wally stayed above and was able to enjoy it all. We spent an hour or so in the evening in Wenceslas Square before going back to the station, collecting our luggage and finding our train.

When the train arrived, the culture shock was immense. I am quite sure that the carriages pre-dated 1939. There was also the problem of the 'single-sex sleepinks'. With great reluctance, I found my allotted sleeping compartment, in which three females of uncertain nationality were already installed. At this point, Wally acted with great enterprise and even courage, by asking the steward if there was a vacant sleeping compartment for two. I was concerned that this might be regarded as a subversive action and possibly a punishable offence, but the steward did not demur, merely beckoning us to follow him along the train. Gathering my suitcase and hat-box, I retreated backwards from my compartment, nodding to my three companions in a manner which I hoped conveyed my delight at having met them – albeit somewhat briefly – and my apologies for leaving them in such haste. The steward led us along the train, produced a key, unlocked a door and ushered us into a compartment for two. He obviously had no qualms about 'mixed sleepinks'.

It was still only 8.30 p.m. and, with over an hour of daylight left, I wanted to sit up for a while and see some of the countryside, but the bunk beds were already in position and it would, I felt, be asking too much of our steward to convert them back to seats. I inspected the bunks more closely. They were made of some sturdy board with a covering of leatherette, a product that pre-dated vinyl by several decades. The only additional items were a very small pillow and a well-worn blanket. This did not encourage me to prepare too thoroughly for bed, but I was reluctant to arrive at our hotel in Warsaw and be mistaken for a refugee, so I decided to remove my trousers at least and fold them neatly on top of my case. We climbed into our respective bunks, with me on the upper one, preparing to read one of the books I had brought with me. However, without any warning the centre light in our compartment went out. I stretched out my hand to find a bedside light, but there was none. On the bunk below, Wally also failed to find any means of illumination. That was it. It was 9 p.m. and all good citizens should be settled down to their sleepinks.

We lay in darkness as the train gathered speed. If the carriages were pre-war, I am sure that the track was laid circa 1870 and had received little, if any, attention since. The train rattled along, seemingly ready to bounce off the tracks at any moment. It was then that I discovered another feature of our sleeping accommodation. Whereas Wally, being over six feet tall, was able to jam himself securely in his bunk with his head resting against one end and his feet firmly planted at the other, I, a mere five feet, four inches, was shuttled interminably back and forth along the length of the bunk, sliding on its leatherette cover as the train swayed alarmingly from side to side, like a solitary pea in an overlarge pod.

Of course, being in complete darkness it was impossible to know what the time was, but at some point in the night there was a loud rapping on our compartment door and a voice shouted 'Passaporta, passaporta!' With foresight, and before we had been plunged into darkness, I had placed our passports in an easily accessible position for just this eventuality. Wally handed them over and in a moment I was being scrutinised by the light of a torch held four inches from my face. It occurred to me that, as my passport photograph was almost ten years old, and as it was now approaching forty-eight hours since my face had made contact either with water or make-up, any resemblance between the photograph and the face now being examined must surely be coincidental. However, the Czech officer seemed satisfied and with a grunt handed them back to us.

We then heard the knock on the compartment next to ours, followed by the demand, 'Passaporta!', but there was no meek acquiescence to this demand. There was the sound of raised voices in a foreign tongue, and scuffles in the corridor. Wally cautiously opened our door a fraction to see what was causing this fracas. It appeared that this compartment was occupied by two Muslim couples who had also apparently overcome the 'no mixed sleepinks' ban but, in this case, the husbands had taken the gravest exception to this close scrutiny of their wives' faces. It was to no avail. I thought I had spotted a gleam of metal near the officer's waistband as he had left our compartment, and in my opinion it is extremely foolhardy to argue too ferociously with a man in uniform carrying a weapon. Our neighbours must have come to the same conclusion, because soon all was quiet again apart from the call of 'Passaporta!' as the officer made his way further along the train.

Twenty minutes later, another call came. 'Paasaporta, passaporta!' Again we went through the same routine – passports produced, torch in the face, satisfied grunt – this time from a Polish officer. I noticed that our neighbours had become aware of the futility of arguing, as there was no repeat of the earlier disturbance. I made another attempt to drift into sleep. Then the call, 'Passaporta, passaporta!' came for a third time. At this point I began to panic. How many borders are there between Czechoslovakia and Poland? I was certain that there was only one on the route we had chosen. Where were we now? Where was Albania? Estonia? Belarus? I longed for an atlas – although, given the total absence of light, it would have been of little use. Passports were produced, grunts given – it was no longer Border Control officers but Immigration officers. At last dawn came, and at 7 a.m. we arrived in Warsaw.

Finding a taxi proved to be easy, and in a very short time and for a remarkably small fare we arrived at our hotel. We went straight to the reception desk and signed in. We were feeling very grubby and in desperate need of a shower and a change of clothes. I asked the receptionist if it would be possible to find us a room where we could shower and change – even if it was not the one allocated to us – but she replied, 'Rooms will be ready at twelve noon.' She then relented slightly and told us that we could go to the dining room and have breakfast. Feeling rather uncomfortable in our dishevelled state, we nevertheless took up her suggestion. The breakfast was excellent and we spun it out until just after nine. Returning to the main reception area I saw that about fifty or sixty men were just leaving, all with their cases, and piling into two coaches outside the hotel. Hearing their American accents, I approached one of them and asked them if they had enjoyed their stay. He was, like most Americans, quite happy to talk and told me that they were all dentists, over from America for an International Convention of Dentists.

The fact that they had all now moved out of their rooms must, I felt, mean that one room could be made available for us within the hour – even after its occupation by an American dentist – and I returned to the receptionist to plead our case. 'Rooms will be ready at twelve noon,' was the reply. Obviously, the concept of customer service had not penetrated her psyche although, given our dirty and unkempt state, it would have surely been wise to have offered us her own room rather than allow us to remain on view in the hotel's main reception area.

Having collected all the tourist brochures available on the counter, I sat stolidly on the sofa immediately in front of her desk and spent the time studying them or reading my book. Wally became so bored that he went for a short walk. Every fifteen minutes I looked up at the clock on the wall behind the receptionist, who made a point of not meeting my gaze. Finally, the two hands of the clock came together on the twelve and the receptionist called out, 'Your room is now ready.' What a relief it was to get into it, have a wash and change. I was convinced it had been ready two hours before, but rules were rules as far as the receptionist was concerned.

One small benefit of having spent three hours idling on the sofa was that I had had plenty of time to study all the tourist literature and had decided that there was a very good city tour leaving from the station at 2 p.m. We jumped into another taxi from the hotel and were soon on board the tour bus with a woman guide who spoke flawless English. We saw many of the magnificent churches, which had been immaculately restored during the communist occupation – there was gold leaf everywhere, with no expense spared to repair the damage caused during the war years. We were taken to the Old Town Market Place and it was explained that, although the entire place had been destroyed between 1939 and 1944, the current buildings had been reconstructed between 1948 and 1953 to look exactly as they had done in the seventeenth century. The builders had done a superb job, and it was difficult to believe that the buildings did not date back to that time.

We then arrived at the Summer Palace. It was beautiful. We were shown the many bullet holes in the outside walls and then taken in and asked to remove our shoes and wear the slippers provided. It was easy to see why this was essential. The floors were superb – all made of wooden marquetry in quite amazing patterns – but easily damaged by high heels or heavy-soled boots. Our guide explained to us that in the years immediately prior to 1939 the building had been a museum and, although the interior had been largely destroyed during the German occupation, with the help of those who had worked there before the war, they were able to refurbish it exactly as it had been. As we were standing in a large reception room with a marquetry floor patterned with leaves and flowers, our guide pointed out the magnificent chandelier which had been remade just like the original one, which had been destroyed during the Second World War. It hung from a ceiling of gloriously intricate plasterwork. She added casually that official receptions were sometimes held there – provided that they were over before dark. This puzzled me, and I asked why this should be. Surely most social events take place in the evening? She shook her head and smiled at me, explaining that they could not hold functions after dark as the candles would dirty the ceiling. I looked more closely at the chandelier. It held real wax candles. I had assumed that they were candle bulbs. I looked out into the hall. To my amazement the wall lights also held candles. I returned to our guide and asked, with genuine interest, why, when they set about restoring this wonderful building, they had not installed electricity. She looked shocked at the thought. It was essential, she said, that everything should be restored exactly as it had been in 1939 and, as at that time it was still in its original eighteenth-century state – when there had certainly been no electricity – the restoration work could not include any such installation. I mentioned – politely – that Buckingham Palace, Chatsworth House and Blenheim Palace had all been built long before Thomas Edison had created the electric lightbulb, and I did not think that any of those buildings suffered in the least from the installation of electricity. She was not convinced by this argument in favour of modernisation.

When we returned to our hotel we found that some friends from Cardiff, also invited to the wedding, had arrived, and we decided to go out for dinner together that evening. We were advised that the best selection of restaurants was in the Old Town Market Place, so we took a taxi straight there. Having checked the various menus outside the restaurants we made our choice and were shown into a basement area lit by candles. I am aware that there are many restaurants in Britain built in the twenty-first century that choose to light their dining area with candles to create a romantic ambience, so I paid little attention to this. The food was excellent.

It was not until we were back in our hotel that I began to wonder whether the Old Town Market Place, along with the Summer Palace, had scorned the installation of any modern amenities when the rebuilding took place. It is to my lasting regret that I did not investigate the toilet facilities. Would I have been led to a hole in the ground at the bottom of the yard, or shown to a small but immaculate area well equipped with gleaming white porcelain? For the sake of their regular patrons and their staff, I sincerely hope it would have been the latter. Restoration can be taken too far.

The wedding itself was all a wedding should be – the sun shone, the bride was beautiful, everyone was happy. After the ceremony, we all spilled out into the sunshine, where we were introduced to a Polish custom where the bride and groom stand on the steps of the church and receive bouquets of flowers from friends and colleagues who were not invited to the wedding, but wanted to express their good wishes for the couple's happiness. This particular young couple was well liked and well known, so the line of donors snaked around the outside of the church as over a hundred people presented their flowers. Traditionally, once the couple and guests leave for the reception, these flowers are taken to local hospitals or residential homes so that many people can benefit from the happy occasion. The next day, a group of us booked a car to take us to Chopin's house at Żelazowa Wola about thirty miles from Warsaw. As it was a Sunday there was a piano concert and we were able to enjoy the music while exploring the gardens. Then it was time for us to leave.

Warsaw station on a Sunday evening leaves much to be desired. We noted with interest, but no concern, that there was absolutely no means of obtaining either food or drink – not even a machine dispensing Coca-Cola. There was also nowhere to sit. There were plenty of seats, but each one was occupied by a young person heavily under the influence of either drink or drugs, and sleeping soundly. To my alarm, another group of young people were urging one of their number, a young girl, to walk along a narrow rail at the half-landing of a massive flight of stone steps. Had she slipped she would have fallen twenty feet on to concrete. I was all for going to pull her off, but Wally pointed out that her companions might not take kindly to having their entertainment curtailed and may just decide to throw me off instead. We thought it would be prudent to remove ourselves from that area and began to look for the departures board.

It was here that we hit something of a problem. There were two boards and our common-sense told us that one was showing departures and the other was showing arrivals – but which was which? In all the other countries we had visited, the words for both arrivals and departures were sufficiently similar to the English as to cause no confusion whatsoever. Polish, however, makes great use of the letter 'Z', and the jumble of letters on display gave no clue as to which one we should be focusing upon. We carefully studied both boards, aware that once the word 'Cologne' appeared we would probably find our platform and our train. Alas, no such word appeared.

We then decided to tackle the problem from another angle. We scanned each board for the time at which our train was due to depart. We found just such a time but the train appeared to be either departing for or arriving from 'Köln'. In the absence of any better alternative, we made our way to the platform listed, where we found a splendid German train clearly indicating that it was going to Köln or, for the more ignorant non-German travellers, to Cologne, and on production of our tickets, a steward led us to our sleeping compartment. He assured us that once we were ready to settle for the night, we were to ring him so that he could arrange our beds. He also took charge of our passports. It seemed that German train passengers were exempt from the facial inspection that had been such a feature on the Polish train. After a good night's sleep we were woken by our steward who, with a magic touch, converted our beds back into comfortable seats with a table for our breakfast, which was also excellent. With Germanic efficiency our train arrived in Brussels exactly on time, and the Eurostar also played its part in departing Brussels and arriving in London precisely as scheduled. Even our westbound British train did not let us down, and we were home in excellent time. Mission accomplished.

Chapter 21

2000 – To Italy by plane

Two years later, in 2000, our daughter, Helen, took up a teaching post in Italy in the small town of Lecco which is situated on the shores of Lake Lecco, which flows into Lake Como. It is a very pretty small town surrounded by the Alps and Helen was anxious that I should visit her there at the earliest opportunity. The small cut-price airlines were offering very competitive rates at the time, so I elected to fly with Buzz out of Stansted direct to Milan.

The outward journey went very smoothly. Helen met me at Milan on the Friday evening and we spent an enjoyable Saturday looking around Lecco, meeting some of her new friends and work colleagues. On Sunday we drove to the ancient walled city of Bergamo which we found both beautiful and interesting. I left Lecco early on Monday morning as Helen had to work, and took the train to Milan Centrale station. Leaving my small overnight bag in the luggage office, I made my way by underground to the Duomo di Milano, or Milan Cathedral, where I spent a couple of hours, first looking around the inside of the cathedral and then taking the lift up to the roof. It was truly spectacular. Every single part of the building is constructed in pale pink marble – even the roof slabs are of the same marble, and each conceivable suitable space has a carving in marble of some kind or another – a saint, a cherub, flowers, leaves, fruit. There were very few visitors there at the time, but I was joined by a young American couple who also marvelled at the wonderful workmanship. The young man expressed the view that if it were constructed today in the United States, it would probably cost more than their entire Gross National Product. I told him that I, coming from the nation which built the Millennium Dome to mark the year 2000, would be wise not to comment.

Leaving the cathedral, I made my way to La Scala where a 'walk-on' rehearsal was in progress. I stayed to watch for half an hour or so – it was quite fascinating to see the singers all in sweaters and jeans being directed around the stage while the words were read to them by a production assistant sitting in the stalls. I debated whether I should have some lunch in Milan or head off to the airport. My flight was due to leave at 4 p.m. and it was just after noon. However, being uncertain how long the taxi journey might take, I decided that I should return to the station, collect my bag and go straight to the airport, where I would have some lunch.

The taxi journey was shorter than I had anticipated, and soon after 1 p.m. I found myself standing beside the Buzz check-in desk over which a sign stated that it would open at 2 p.m. I went off to the cafeteria for a light lunch. Returning to the check-in desk promptly at 2 p.m., I found that waiting in front of me were six of the largest men I have ever seen. They were not especially tall, but they were extremely wide. They were also carrying two enormous silver trophies. One, a rose bowl, must have had a diameter of almost two feet. The other was a cup which, on its plinth, stood three feet high. Ever curious, I asked them what these were, and I was told – with considerable pride – that they were the British weightlifting team and that they had just won the World Championship. I congratulated them and then the check-in desk opened and we all booked on to our flight. It was still only a little after 2 p.m. so I headed off to a rather pleasant coffee house which I had noted earlier, and spent an hour or so sipping coffee and sampling a very good Italian cake. By then it was approaching 3.30 p.m. so I thought I may as well make my way to the boarding gate. As I reached it, I noticed that the flight departure time was reading 5 p.m. I checked my ticket – definitely 4 p.m. – oh well, I thought, so there was an hour's delay. I settled down with my book. Other passengers joined me, including my new-found weightlifting friends. There were a few grumbles over the impending delay but for £59 return there seemed little point in becoming too hysterical. At 4.45 p.m. we were all advised to board the plane. We did so, the steps were removed and the doors were closed. Five o'clock came and went, as did 5.15 p.m. Then it was 5.30 p.m. and still we sat in an immobile aircraft. At 5.35 p.m. our British stewardess made an announcement informing us that there was a fault on the plane and they were telephoning London to ask what they should do. I had a mental flash of London's advice: 'See that little screw, third from the left? Get a screwdriver and…' or, even more alarmingly, 'Have you got a piece of string handy?'

At 5.45 p.m. London's advice came through: 'Take all the passengers off the plane.' All one hundred and four of us trooped back to our original boarding gate. The British crew accompanied us and told us that we would now be handed over to the airline's Italian ground staff, who would keep us informed of any progress. With a cheery 'good luck' they all melted away to sample the delights of an evening in Milan while we sat despondently around waiting for the next development.

This turned out to be the appearance of a very pretty, fragile Italian girl whose command of the English language left much, if not everything, to be desired. First she gave an announcement in Italian – the passengers, I estimated, were approximately half Italian and half British. Judging by the expressions on the Italians' faces it was not all good news. She then attempted the same announcement in English. Assisted by some bilingual passengers, we eventually got the message. An engineer was flying from Britain on the next Buzz flight, which was due to arrive in Milan at 7.30 p.m. He would repair the fault and the plane would then take off for Stansted. It seemed to me that any fault capable of grounding the plane must surely take at least an hour to repair, and I rather hoped that the repair would be followed with some sort of test – without any passengers on board. This, I calculated, would make our time of departure 9.30 p.m. at the earliest.

The grumbles gained momentum. Our fragile staff member tried another tack. Anyone who did not have essential business in Britain the next day should volunteer to spend the night in Milan, courtesy of Buzz Airlines. Would all those prepared to do so move to the adjoining boarding gate? The result of this request bore a startling resemblance to a game of musical statues at a children's party. Not one of the hundred and four people gathered there moved. The Italian girl was almost in tears and finally fled from the scene. Then, like a human tornado, a more senior member of ground staff appeared. She was a sturdily built soul, wearing thick tights and flat shoes. In faultless English (and presumably in faultless Italian too) she informed us that there were twenty available seats on the next Buzz flight back to Stansted, which departed at 8.15 p.m., and they had also negotiated forty-six seats on a BA flight leaving for Heathrow at 8 p.m. She instructed her sensitive assistant, who had now rejoined us, to make a list of all those prepared to fly to Heathrow. This was wonderful news for me, as it would make the final stage of my journey so much easier, and I rushed forward at once. 'I'll go to Heathrow, I'll volunteer.' My name was noted. After me came a flood of passengers all more than happy to travel to Heathrow. The weightlifting team came forward although, as their cars were at Stansted, they were less than happy with the arrangement but, being promised a taxi to deliver them to Stansted, decided to throw in their lot with BA.

It was soon evident that the volunteers for the BA flight far exceeded the number of seats available, and our delicate friend began again to show signs of distress. Just then the human tornado reappeared, telling us all that we must collect our luggage from the carousel hall. Now I only had my overnight bag which I had kept with me but, concerned that I may miss out on the next stage in the proceedings, I followed her obediently as she set a rapid pace to the carousel hall. While luggage was being collected, her assistant must have explained her dilemma about more people volunteering for the BA flight and the more limited Buzz flight than there were seats available. Accordingly, our efficient guide decided that the fairest way to allocate places was to take us all in the order in which we had originally checked in. We returned to our former waiting area and a list was produced. The tearful assistant was to call out the names as they appeared on the list and in turn we were to state whether we wanted the Buzz flight or the BA flight. Obviously the last thirty-eight checked in would have to stay overnight in Milan. Again I was delighted – secure in the knowledge that I had been the seventh person to check in, immediately after the six weightlifters, and could comfortably secure a seat on the flight to Heathrow.

The roll call began.

'Alberto?'

'Heathrow.'

'Angelotti?'

'Stansted.'

'Arthur?'

'Stansted.'

'Bartoli?'

'Heathrow.'

'Berini?'

'Heathrow.'

The British woman doctor standing next to me hissed, 'That's not in order of check-in, that's alphabetical order!', and, indeed, those names did not sound much like the British weightlifting team.

Even so, I felt some degree of relief as I had used my full surname and knew that I must surely be called while there was still ample room on the Heathrow flight. On went the roll call.

'Brown.'

'Stansted, but what about my daughter and grandson? Their surname is Taylor.' There was much flicking over of computerised sheets until these names were found and duly ticked.

'Colognese.'

'Heathrow.'

'Compton?'

'Heathrow – but what about my girlfriend, Miss Samson?'

My name came next, and I was duly marked off for Heathrow. However, at this point there was an uprising in the ranks, started, not surprisingly by the Smiths, Thomases and Williams, in the group who saw any prospect of a return to British soil that evening fading before their eyes. The situation could have taken a very nasty turn, but was saved by the reappearance of the tornado who swept into the hall and announced that the BA check-in desk was about to close and we were to follow her immediately.

Regardless of whether their name had been called or even whether Heathrow was a viable option for them, all one hundred and four passengers gathered their possessions and followed hot on her heels. She could certainly move. Those with more than hand luggage were soon left behind, and although the weightlifters got off to a good start, they were not really built for sustained running, especially when encumbered by two large silver trophies, Thus, although they were ahead of me in the hall, I easily overtook them when we ascended a long flight of stairs. With only one small bag, I made excellent time on the flat, passing several others, and arrived at the check-in desk eighth in line. The check-in was cursory and we were exhorted to run to the departure gate; very soon all forty six (including the weightlifters) had boarded – perhaps they were able to use their bulk to their advantage in the final scrum at the desk.

We took off as planned at 8 p.m. On arriving at Heathrow two hours later, 9 p.m. British time, I turned on my mobile phone. It rang immediately. It was Helen calling from Italy. Hearing the babble of conversation in the background she said, 'Oh good, you're on the train to Cardiff.'

'No,' I replied, 'I've just landed at Heathrow.'

There was a long silence and then Helen said, 'But Mum, you were flying into Stansted!'

'Don't even ask,' was my reply.

It might have been thought that the above represented quite sufficient inconvenience for one day, but there was more to come. Arriving at Heathrow Terminal 2, I took the Heathrow Express to Paddington Station. This train runs every fifteen minutes, and takes fifteen minutes, and thus I was at Paddington shortly after 9.30 p.m. with just time for a coffee with a couple of biscuits in a pleasant cafe before boarding the 10 p.m. train to Cardiff. When I got on the train it was fairly full, but I found a comfortable seat with my back to the engine and opened my book. In fact, the train did not leave until 10.25 p.m. but as this was not long after the Hatfield rail disaster, which had been in October 2000, disruptions and delays were not uncommon. The majority of the passengers left the train at Reading and a further number got off at Didcot. In fact, when we left Swindon station I was the only passenger remaining in my coach.

I sat back, content in the knowledge that the next stop would be Bristol Parkway and from there it was a mere half an hour or so to Cardiff. I must have dropped off to sleep, for I woke just as we were pulling out of a station. I noticed that a young couple had got into my coach and were standing near the doorway. Glancing out of the window, it occurred to me that the scenery looked remarkably rural for Bristol Parkway. I got up from my seat and made my way towards my new travel companions.

'Excuse me,' I began, 'but could you tell me what station that was?'

It transpired that they were French. 'Cheep-un-arm,' the young man replied, which my sleep-befuddled brain eventually unscrambled as Chippenham. Now, I knew without doubt that Chippenham was not on the list of stations posted on the departure board at Paddington, neither did it feature on the list of stations posted on the side of the train at the time of its departure. I addressed another question to the young pair. 'Could you tell me where this train is going, please?'

They both looked a trifle disconcerted but replied, 'Soo-am-say-er.' Which, after a few moments, I unscrambled to mean Swansea – a town fifty miles west of Cardiff. Relieved at this, I returned to my seat. The French couple did not attempt to venture further into the coach, remaining close to the door – obviously ready for a quick getaway from this lunatic woman who did not even know what train she was on.

We pulled into another station – Bath – good news. Definitely closer to Cardiff – even if not on the main Cardiff–London line. The young pair left the train here and once again I was alone in my coach, but I felt we were now getting very close to Bristol Parkway. I must have dropped off to sleep again, although I could vaguely recall an announcement to the effect that we were arriving at that station. Any moment now we must be entering the Severn Tunnel – if we had not already gone through it. Again I glanced out of the window. After a few moments, an icy fear grasped me. When we left Paddington and indeed when we left Bath, I knew perfectly well that I was sitting with my back to the engine. Now, however, I seemed to be facing it. I fixed my eyes on a light in a house across some fields a little way ahead. There was no doubt about it; it was getting nearer and now we had gone past it. There seemed to be only one explanation. An announcement had been made at Parkway to the effect that all passengers for Wales must change trains – and I had slept through it.

Panic swept through me. Where were we headed? Back to Paddington, perhaps. A worse scenario occurred to me. We were heading for a siding where the train and I would languish until morning. I felt that immediate action was called for. I leaped from my seat and began to rapidly make my way into the next coach, going towards the engine. This was empty of all passengers, as was the next, and the one after that. Having reached the coach immediately behind the engine, I had no clear idea of what action I could take. Banging on the back of the coach seemed fairly futile. For a wild moment I considered trying to climb out of the window to attract the driver's attention.

Fortunately, I was spared from any such decision since, coming towards me from the end of the train, was the ticket collector.

'Where are we?' I asked imploringly.

He looked at me sorrowfully. 'I wish I knew,' he replied. 'We keep being diverted due to line repairs.'

'But we are going to Cardiff?' I persisted.

'Oh yes,' was the comforting rejoinder, and then to further assuage any remaining doubts he added, 'There's a young man in the last coach who is going to Swansea.' So there we were – the train driver, the ticket collector, the young man destined for Swansea and I in a train that was 'wandering lonely as a cloud' around the highways and byways of the Western region railway network.

We arrived in Cardiff at 2.10 a.m. As I made my way along the platform to the stairs and the train began to move off, I spotted the young man, still hopeful of reaching Swansea, and I wondered what further diversionary delights awaited him.

Would he see the moon over Merthyr? Or the dawn rise over Aberdare? As for me, it was a taxi and home.

Chapter 22

2005 – To Italy by train

By 2005, five years later, Helen, who by now was working in London, married her Italian boyfriend, Livio, who was also working in London. The wedding took place in Cardiff with the reception at our home. Forty-seven Italian friends and relations made the journey from Italy, but a number of Livio's older relations were not well enough to undertake the trip, and so it was decided that a second reception would be held in his home town of Bari two months later.

The challenge of planning our journey was made considerably easier with the aid of the internet. Wally and I would travel to London on the Wednesday, take the early-afternoon Eurostar to Paris, Gare du Nord, and after a two-hour break in Paris, take the overnight sleeper – Il Palatino – from Paris to Rome. We booked a two-berth sleeping compartment on this train – there was no problem with 'mixed sleepinks' for the Italians. This schedule allowed for a two-hour break in Rome – perfect for enjoying an early lunch before taking our train on to Bari, a journey of five hours, and we would arrive in Bari early on Thursday evening. Helen and Livio would take an early-morning flight from London on Friday and join up with us mid-morning. We also decided to take advantage of the trip by making a three-day stopover in Rome on our return.

The journey began well enough, as they always do. We arrived in Paris on time and enjoyed a coffee in a nearby cafe before taking a taxi to Gare du Bercy where our train was waiting. We were escorted to our compartment by an obliging steward who assured us that he would prepare our beds for us while we were at dinner. The train left promptly at 8.30 p.m. and we made our way to the dining car where we enjoyed a very good meal. Returning to our compartment at 11 p.m., we were a little disconcerted to find that our beds were not yet in position. Wally suggested that we might try to put them up ourselves, but I felt that this operation may well require an element of training and, no doubt, if we were to attempt it ourselves we would be in breach of some health and safety regulation. I was reasonably sure that the long arm of Euro bureaucracy had extended to Italy. We waited twenty minutes or so, during which time I made my way along the corridor both of our coach and the adjoining one, but there was not a steward in sight.

I was now becoming rather annoyed, reflecting that we had paid marginally more for the privilege of sleeping overnight on this train than we would have done for a double room in a four-star hotel, and our opportunities for using this facility were rapidly fading. Realising that the train was stationary, I opened a window and stuck my head out. I saw seven or eight stewards further along the platform, all enjoying their cigarettes. I opened the door at the end of the coach and headed along the platform to them. I could not see our own steward among them, but tried to explain our problem in my singularly inadequate Italian. 'Potrebbe gentilmente preparare i nostri letti?' ('Please could you prepare our beds?') Finally one of the group came forward and explained that, although he was not the steward for our coach, he would assist us.

In a flash, with a deft flick of his wrist two beds materialised and as he left he made what I thought was a strange remark: 'Make sure your door is locked.' We wouldn't have considered going to sleep without locking the door but we thanked him for his concern, and Wally locked the door with a resounding click. Our sleeping compartment was comfortable, with a small wash-basin in the corner furthest from the door, and, before I climbed into my bunk I carefully placed my handbag on the floor beneath the window directly opposite the door. It was a large handbag with a shoulder strap and six or seven pockets both inside and out, which I had used to separate the various items I was carrying – wallet in one, mobile phone in another, reading glasses, small wallet with further cash, lipstick and comb, passport wallet containing a credit card for emergency use in the others. It was a very useful bag for travelling.

It was now well past midnight, so I climbed into my bunk and listened to my audio book for some time before turning it off and settling to sleep. Breakfast commenced at 7.30 a.m., and soon after 7 a.m. Wally woke me to ask if I was going for breakfast. He is not a breakfast person, but it is the one meal of the day which is absolutely essential for me. A bowl of cereal or slice of toast – rarely both – and I can survive quite happily for twelve hours or more. Thus I set off to the dining car and enjoyed a simple but adequate breakfast for 5 euros which I had in the purse section of my wallet. I came back to our compartment and we spent the next two or three hours reading, doing crosswords and looking out at the scenery which, I noticed, we were not passing at any great speed. At about 10.30 a.m. an announcement was made to the effect that due to a cow on the line? avalanche? revolution? (my Italian is rudimentary), we would be arriving in Rome one and a half hours late.

This called for a revision in our plans for lunch, as we would now have less than half an hour between train connections. However, once in Rome we made a quick visit to the delicatessen at the station and stocked up on sandwiches and drinks to take us comfortably through the last leg of our journey. I went to the cash desk to pay, and discovered to my astonishment that the 100 euros which I had known, without a shadow of doubt, was there after I had paid for our dinner the previous evening was nowhere to be seen and, furthermore, the two credit cards which had certainly been there had also mysteriously disappeared. Deeply worried by this, I ferreted further into one of the other pockets which should have held a small wallet with 400 euros – it was also empty. Finally I took out my passport wallet where, tucked well away, should have been my final, emergency use, credit card. The wallet was there, the passport was there, but the credit card had gone. I could not believe it – my bag had never been left unattended, and for a pickpocket to search in all these various pockets in my presence would have required a degree of deftness which would have defied the most highly skilled Fagin.

Fortunately Wally had some loose coins in his pocket which proved sufficient for our purchases. Wally thought that we should inform the police on the station but, with less than ten minutes before our train was due to leave, and given my poor command of the language, I felt that we would be better getting to Bari and trying to report it there. During the five-hour journey to Bari we mulled over how these losses could have occurred. Mercifully, when we arrived at Bari we found that our hotel was just two hundred yards away, directly opposite the station, and so we had no need for a taxi or to face a long walk with our cases. As soon as we arrived in our room we telephoned our son Brendan, asking him to report all three credit cards as stolen and to phone Helen in London and make sure she had sufficient funds in her bank to draw out cash for us for our stay in Bari and in Rome. I did not feel that the two cards left in my wallet – my local library card and my Tesco Clubcard – would be overly useful in trying to obtain cash in Italy.

Ten minutes later, Helen telephoned us. Yes, she would make sure that we had cash, but she added that Livio had told her that we had undoubtedly been drugged in our sleep on the train, which was when my bag had been removed and thoroughly searched for any items of value. This was, she said, apparently quite common. This made me feel much better, as I could now feel totally exonerated from any blame for the loss. Then Brendan telephoned to tell us that the credit-card companies would cover any outgoings on the cards, providing that we could present them with a crime number from the Italian police. With this in mind, as soon as Helen and Livio arrived the next morning we went immediately to the local police station. Helen speaks fluent Italian and explained the whole sequence of events. The police officer began to write it all down painstakingly. When she reached the part of the tale where we had settled into our bunks, his face broke into a wide smile. Raising his right arm, he flicked his forefinger up and down as he was pressing an aerosol spray. 'Il misto. Il misto. Normale, puo capitane,' he assured us. My Italian is far from fluent, but I grasped what he was saying. 'Non in Galles,' I shouted indignantly. 'Non normale. Non accade. Certainement non.' Not in Wales. Not normal. It does not happen. Certainly not. It is probably just as well that my Italian is limited, as what I really wanted to say was, 'What total rubbish. Why don't you do something about it? Call yourselves a police force.' It is quite possible that these remarks may have brought me some form of retribution – which would have spoiled the happy occasion. The police officer gave a Gallic shrug and continued his report. Once he had finished he handed it to us, complete with crime number, so we were free to get on with some sightseeing.

Bari is beautiful and interesting and the reception the next day was a total joy. I do wish, however, that we had been made aware that the meal consisted of eleven courses, as we would not have eaten quite so much of the first three. From a strictly practical point, we felt obliged to miss out the next six, returning with renewed enthusiasm for the last two. After another day of sightseeing on Sunday, Helen and Livio set off for the airport while Wally and I collected our cases from our hotel and crossed the square to catch the 6 p.m. train to Rome. The platform proved to be unexpectedly crowded, bearing more resemblance to a central London Underground station at rush hour than one in a pleasant town in southern Italy on a Sunday evening.

As we stood there, more and more people crowded on, mostly from trains coming up from the south. At around 6.45 p.m. two or three officials appeared on the platform and began herding us to the exit. We had no idea why this was happening, but had little option but to go with the crowd. Eventually we were all assembled outside in the square in front of the station – there must have been six hundred people. Announcements were made in Italian and one or two of our fellow travellers, seeing the bemused expressions on our faces, attempted an explanation. Unfortunately their English was on a par with my Italian and we remained mystified.

Eventually a tall Danish lady took pity on us and, being fluent in both English and Italian, explained that there had been an accident on the line some twenty miles north which had resulted in a death. As a consequence, all rail travel between Bari and Barletta – the next town north on the line – had been suspended. After a further half an hour, two coaches arrived in the square and an announcement was made which the Danish lady again translated for us. It informed us that all passengers wishing to travel north would be taken by coach to the next station (Barletta, thirty miles away) where a train was waiting for them to continue their journey north. This train had, presumably, been on its way south, but had been forced to stop at Barletta and turn round to go back the way it had come. We were also told that passengers on their way to Bari and further south would likewise be brought by coach from Barletta to Bari, where trains which had been making their way north would similarly turn round and head back south.

As I digested this information, I began to work out the mathematics of the problem. I had a certain degree of respect for the rail authorities who had managed to muster two forty-seater coaches on a Sunday evening, and had presumably managed to find a further two heading for Barletta. However, on the basis that, of the six hundred passengers now gathered in the square, probably four hundred were hoping to travel north, that was going to mean five trips for the two coaches. I felt that it would be unlikely that each journey could be made in less than thirty minutes and, adding a further ten minutes for unloading and loading passengers, it would be almost three hours before all four hundred were safely transported to their new departure point. I was also well aware that as we were standing – queuing – on the side of the square farthest from the coaches' departure point, it seemed most unlikely that we would be leaving Bari much before 10 p.m. and, with a five-hour train journey from Barletta to Rome, I could see little prospect us arriving in that city before 3.30 a.m.

We stood dejectedly in the square and considered returning to our hotel for the night, but travelling the next day would make considerable inroads into our time in Rome. At this point it began to rain – not a deluge, just steady light rain that was just as effective at dampening both our clothes and our spirits. Relief came in the form of the Danish lady, who suggested that we might like to share a taxi with her to take us to Barletta. As she explained, there would be a train waiting there, offering both a seat and an opportunity to get out of the rain. We readily fell in with her suggestion and soon were making good time along the road to Barletta.

As we drove along, we told her of our experience with 'il misto'. She did not express shock, or even surprise, and told us a story of a similar incident. She was a widow, an interior designer. She lived in a second-floor apartment ten miles outside Rome and one of her interests was collecting old and rare rugs. Her other passion was her four dogs, who shared the apartment with her. One night she went to bed and, as usual, left her bedroom window open. She explained that this was essential to her as, being Danish, she craved cool fresh air at night. One of her dogs slept in her bedroom and the other three in the hall. I assumed at this point that the rare and valuable rugs were hung upon walls, as I knew from my own experience that dogs do not improve the appearance of even cheap and cheerful rugs. When she woke in the morning she found that every rug had been stolen, including one from her bedroom. She knew immediately that she had been gassed through her open window, giving the thieves ample opportunity to remove every rug while she and the dogs slept soundly through the intrusion. Hearing this story, I felt that we had got off lightly. I have no idea of the value of the rugs, but I was fairly confident that it was rather more than the 500 euros which we had lost.

There was a train waiting at Barletta and, as soon as every seat had been taken, it set off for Rome. We arrived at our hotel at 2.45 a.m., but when we began to make our apologies for our late arrival we were waved aside. The accident had been the main news headline all evening and the hotel management was well aware that we would be very late in arriving. We had three very pleasant days sightseeing in Rome and then once again boarded Il Palatino. I placed the last of my euros – courtesy of Helen – into the pocket of my passport holder which I hung around my neck and tucked firmly under my T-shirt, then settled down to sleep face-down on my bunk. My last waking thought before I drifted off to sleep was 'Let them just try.' They didn't, and the rest of our journey was uneventful, with the Eurostar behaving perfectly and our home connection right on time.

Robert Louis Stevenson wrote, 'To travel hopefully is a better thing than to arrive', and so we continue to travel hopefully and usually arrive – although not always at the expected time and, on occasion, not even at the expected place.